Faith
Active
in Love

An Investigation of the Principles
Underlying Luther's Social Ethics

....

George Wolfgang Forell

Augsburg Publishing House
Minneapolis, Minnesota

*To my parents
who first taught me the meaning of
Faith Active in Love*

Foreword

Can one course of action be called good and its alternative evil? If so, what determines that one is good and the other not good? Moreover, does *the good* remain constant, the same for all people in all ages? Is there a private good which is different from a social good? These are all ethical questions.

But the most perplexing ethical question of all is this: Granting that there is such a thing as *the good*, how can a man who knows the good be made to do the good at whatever cost to himself?

This volume by Professor Forell is a study of how Dr. Luther and his Reformation associates came to grips with the ethical questions and, above all, with the question of ethical motivation. It is a book on theological ethics.

The great Reformer and the church which bears his name have often been charged with ethical quietism. Reviving the great teaching of the New Testament that a man finds favor and reconciliation with God, not through works but by grace through faith, Luther is accused of leading Christendom away from ethical concern and discipline into a sterile world of theological speculation and ecclesiastical formalism. Dr. Forell's volume, though not exhaustive, is a clear documentary refutation of this misunderstanding of the operation of grace and faith. Far from being ethically impotent, Christian faith finds its life only in a radical love of neighbor and brother. In fact, one is almost led to the conclusion that without faith (which is God's transforming work in the heart of man), all talk of the good life is illusory.

This volume is more than an attempt to vindicate the Reformation in the field of ethics. More important, it is a study which will be for every careful reader a work of utmost contemporary relevance.

ALVIN N. ROGNESS

Acknowledgments

The discussion of Luther's social ethics in this country has been characterized by an almost exclusive dependence on secondary sources in general and Ernst Troeltsch's massive study of *The Social Teachings of the Christian Churches* in particular.

Whatever value these pages may have will depend almost entirely on the attempted injection of more of Luther's own words into the discussion of his social views. The large number of quotations and footnotes is the result of an effort to let Luther speak for himself on this controversial subject.

The author is indebted to many people for inspiration, criticism, and help. They are his teachers, Professor Josef Bohatec of the University of Vienna, Professor Theodore G. Tappert of the Lutheran Theological Seminary at Philadelphia, Professors Otto Piper and Joseph Hromadka of Princeton Theological Seminary, and Professors Robert Hastings Nichols, Reinhold Niebuhr, John T. McNeill, and John C. Bennett of Union Theological Seminary, New York. He has been enlightened by his colleagues in the Lutheran Social Ethics Study Group of Valparaiso University and stimulated by his associates on the faculty of Gustavus Adolphus College. He owes much to his students, whose searching questions forced him to try to clarify his position. And he is forever in debt to his wife for her help and encouragement when such assistance was most needed.

Acknowledgment is made to the following publishers for their kind permission to quote from copyrighted publications: Abingdon Cokesbury Press, Nashville, Tennessee: John T. McNeill, *Unitive Protestantism;* Augustana Book Concern, Rock Island, Illinois: Einar Billing, *Our Calling;* Columbia University Press, New York: William Lunt, *Papal Revenues in the Middle Ages;* Harcourt, Brace and Company, New York: R. H. Tawney,

Religion and the Rise of Capitalism; Houghton Mifflin Company, Boston: William M. McGovern, *From Luther to Hitler;* The Macmillan Company, New York: *Encyclopaedia of the Social Sciences;* McGraw-Hill Book Company, New York: George Catlin, *Story of the Political Philosophers;* Oxford University Press, New York: Arnold J. Toynbee, *A Study of History;* Charles Scribner's Sons, New York: D. M. Baillie, *God Was in Christ* and Eduard Heimann, *Freedom and Order;* The United Lutheran Publication House, Philadelphia: *The Works of Martin Luther.*

G. W. F.

St. Peter, Minnesota
Ascension Day, 1954

ABBREVIATIONS USED IN TEXT AND FOOTNOTES

E.A.	Erlanger Ausgabe, Erlangen Edition of Luther's Works.
Tr. Lenker	The Writings of Dr. Martin Luther in English translation, edited by J. N. Lenker.
Tr. Loy	Luther's House-Postil in English translation edited by M. Loy.
Phila. Ed.	The Philadelphia Edition of Luther's works.
St. L.	St. Louis Edition of Luther's works.
W.A.	Weimarer Ausgabe, Weimar Edition of Luther's works.
W.A.B.	Weimar Edition of Luther's letters.
W.A.T.	Weimar Edition of Luther's table-talk.

All translations are the author's unless otherwise indicated in the footnotes. When the Lenker or Loy editions have been mentioned in the notes, they have been used by the author for purposes of comparison.

Contents

I. INTRODUCTION

It is customary to date the beginning of the Reformation from the 31st of October, 1517. When the Augustinian friar Martin Luther nailed to the door of the Castle Church of Wittenberg his ninety-five theses discussing the power and efficacy of indulgences, his action proved to be one with the most far-reaching religious, political, and economic consequences. While the historical importance of Luther's action is generally recognized, the fact that the act was an expression of the young professor's feeling of social responsibility has often been forgotten. The high-pressure sale of indulgences as practiced by Tetzel under the supervision of the Fugger banking house did not affect Luther personally. He had known for some time that "the whole life of believers should be repentance."[1] To take this public action and to call the attention of the learned world to the abuses of the Dominican salesmen of counterfeit salvation was an attempt on the part of Luther to bring his ethical standards of right and wrong to bear upon society. Thus the Reformation began with an action which must be called "social." Here lies the difference between Luther and some of the men who had arrived at very similar theological insights but had let these matters remain in the realm of "individual ethics."[2] In Luther the personal conviction created a feeling of social responsibility which expressed itself in the public proclamation of the ninety-five theses. To be sure, Luther did not and could not anticipate the tremendous effects that his action would have. It was not his plan to bring the matter before the general public by means of his theses. But as his simultaneous letters to the Archbishop of Mainz and the Bishop of Brandenburg clearly indicate, he was concerned with the welfare of the people. He feared that "through these false fables and worthless promises" (of the indulgence preachers) the common people were being led astray.[3]

Unlike a medieval mystic or a saintly hermit, who enjoys his personal relationship to God and cares little if the world about him perishes, Luther's entire life was social action, i.e., a conscious attempt to influence the society of which he

. . . .

[1] Weimarer Ausgabe (W.A.), 1, 233, 10 (Indulgence Disputation, 1517). Cf. Philadelphia Edition, I, 29: "Our Lord and Master Jesus Christ, when he said Poenitentiam agite (Matthew 4:17), willed that the whole life of believers should be repentance."

[2] E.g., Wessel Gansfort (1420-89), who by training and conviction had been in a very similar position. Luther himself felt that if he had read Wessel before the controversy concerning the indulgences had begun, his enemies could have claimed that "Luther took everything from Wessel, because we agree so fully." (W.A., 10, II, 316 ff, Preface to the Letters of Wessel, 1522.) Luther realized that the difference between Wessel and

was a part and the orders or organisms which in his opinion made up this society.

It would be very strange indeed if a person so active in society and so deeply involved in social action would have no ethical principle to direct him in these activities. From 1517 to 1546 Luther tried to guide in their religious as well as social decisions all who would listen. His last action in life was social action, an attempt to arbitrate a conflict about some mining property between the counts of Mannsfeld. Under these circumstances, an assertion that Luther had no social ethics would take away the motivation for all these efforts. Only if Luther believed that social action is imperative, and that the Christian has insights which give him the opportunity to help others to live in this world, can Luther's life be explained, for it was from beginning to end a life of social action. The question arises: Is it possible to discover the principles motivating Luther's social ethics? The following pages are an attempt to prove that this is possible and to describe the relation of these principles to the standards of Luther's social ethics.

The principles underlying Luther's social ethics are more important for an understanding of the social-ethical statements Luther made than these statements themselves. While these particular assertions were often colored by the acci-

. . . .

himself might have been that fear of the resulting conflict prevented Wessel from a public proclamation of his views (Ibid., 317, 18: "I wonder what ill fortune prevented it that this most Christian author [Gansfort] never became known; per chance the reason was that he lived without war and bloodshed."). Cf. Edward W. Miller and Jared W. Scudder: *Wessel Gansfort, Life and Writings,* New York, 1917, I, 232.

[3] W.A. Briefe, 1, No. 48, 110 ff. (October 31, 1517). Cf. Phila. Ed., I, 25 ff., e.g., 26: "Thus souls committed to your care, Good Father, are taught to their death, and the strict account which you must render for all such grows and increases. For this reason I have no longer been able to keep quiet. . . ."

dental social, political, and economic circumstances of his turbulent age, the underlying principles had their source directly in the theological convictions of the reformer. Thus a mere collection and collation of these particular assertions apart from the principles that motivate them will prove meaningless.

Even a cursory reading of Luther's many writings reveals the fact that a simple accumulation of Luther's opinions on the various contemporary social problems can only lead to greater confusion. Luther's works after 1517 were of necessity of a polemical nature since the author was the most controversial figure in Europe. Luther was involved in conflicts with people of all types of social-ethical convictions, from the Roman pope to the communistic peasant revolutionaries. The character of the group he addressed did not fail to influence the specific expression of his views. Thus it is possible to quote from one particular work and receive an impression of his social views totally different from that given by another work written under different circumstances.

For this reason it is of the utmost importance to establish the principles which underlie all of Luther's utterances on social ethics and which serve to explain the specific attitudes he took when social-ethical problems confronted him.

In the following the effort has been made to relate Luther's social ethics to his theological method. For Luther ethics was the practical expression of theological method. His ethics is incomprehensible apart from the theological method which created it. Since all of Luther's thought is centered in his personal discovery of the forgiveness of sins through God's gracious justification, an understanding of his social ethics demands that the lines that lead from this central point of his thought to his social ethics be clearly drawn.

Similarly, it can also be shown that Luther's social ethics is an integral part of his Christian ethics, that it is impossible to separate his social ethics from his individual ethics in such a manner that the former becomes a mere afterthought dominated by naturalistic and sub-Christian notions. Luther's general ethical principle is an essential factor for

14

the understanding of his social ethics.

But probably the most controversial aspect of Luther's social ethics is his practical approach to the problems of society. Here it is important to realize that it was indeed a "practical" approach, and that Luther was quite aware of the positive character of society as a means through which the Christian can serve God. Far from merely depreciating the family and the state as repressive means to keep sin in check, Luther saw in them the outgrowth of God's creative orders as they pre-date the fall of man and the entrance of sin into human relations. For an understanding of Luther's practical principle of social ethics, it is basic to understand his teaching of the two realms of human existence, the secular and the spiritual, and to keep firmly in mind that the very word *secular* creates a semantic problem in our time. For Luther the secular realm was also God's realm, and modern naturalistic and agnostic connotations of this term tend to confuse the meaning of Luther's thought.

The danger of reading Luther from the philosophical point of view of twentieth-century man does not only appear in the domain of semantics. Luther's entire social ethics is developed against the background of faith in the immediately impending invasion and transformation of the world of social ethics by the coming kingdom of God. In the background of all his utterances stands his firm belief in the imminent day of Jesus Christ. It is Luther's eschatology which supplies the limiting principle to his social ethical thought. This human society with its political, social, and economic problems is passing away. That we live in a dying world is Luther's firm conviction.

Luther's social ethics must be understood in relation to his theological method, his basic ethical standards, his practical understanding of the structure of the world, and the eschatological background of all life. Apart from these basic aspects of his thought his utterances must seem meaningless and contradictory. These principles constitute the framework upon which his social ethics has been erected. That such a framework exists is the contention of this presentation.

15

II. THE PROBLEM

In view of the obvious social interest of Luther as he demonstrated it in action all during his life and as it is recorded in many of his writings, it should seem easy to show the existence and the content of his social ethics. But in a discussion of Luther's thought on any subject, the fact of the controversial nature of his personality complicates matters greatly.

A look at the literature reveals that nowhere is Luther's thought the object of a more heated controversy than in the field of ethics. It was exactly at this point that Roman Catholic historians leveled their attack against Luther. In

. . . .

[1] H. Denifle, *Luther und Luthertum,* Mainz, 1904-09, I, 744, 763 ff, II, 194 ff. This interpretation of Luther in terms of moral corruption has been summarized by Denifle in *Luther in rationalistischer und christlicher Beleuchtung,* Mainz, 1904, pp. 33 ff. "What does Luther mean to the true Christian? He is an ordinary, yes, perhaps even an extraordinary man of revolt, a revolutionary who passed through his age like a demon, and who ruthlessly stamped down what a millennium before him had venerated. He is a seducer who pulled hundreds of thousands along with him into his fateful errors. He is a false prophet who in his contradictory doctrine and sinful life proclaimed the very opposite of that which one expects of a man sent by God. He is a liar and deceiver who with the slogan of Christian liberty and by sacrificing all Christian restraints, pulled many fools along with him." Hartmann Grisar, S.J., a far more sophisticated Roman Catholic biographer, interpreted Luther less in terms of devil possession (as had been the common practice) and more in terms of "neuroses" and "psychoses," and thus proved a somewhat more effective critic of Luther. Grisar's considered judgment of the social influence of Luther was: "In the course of history even evil seed may produce new and useful elements for further development, if this is God's plan." This view makes greater (if grudging) concessions to the actual historical development. However, Grisar proceeds later to show that, "practically,"

the nineteenth century, H. Denifle, a Dominican biographer of Luther, claimed that because of the Reformation vice and immorality increased beyond anything that had been previously experienced. Denifle insisted that Luther's gospel proved to be a school of sins and vices. Furthermore, he claimed that the theory of evolution, agnosticism, immanentism, relativism, subjectivism, and the Kantian ideas of autonomy—in fact the entire modern world view—were direct descendants of Luther. "Lutheranism," he said, "stands everywhere for these modern ideas and considers every attack against them an attack against itself."[1]

It was also in the field of ethics and social ethics in particular, that modern socialism and Marxism found Luther wanting.[2]

. . . .

Luther's social teachings led to the domination of the church by the state, the collapse of education, reduction of charity for the poor, an inferior view of vocation, and a pessimistic view of all walks of life. It is interesting to note that Grisar speaks of an exaggeration in the application of the principles of the Bible when Luther criticizes the flourishing capitalism of his time. Against Luther, Grisar emphasizes the progressive views of Roman Catholicism with respect to the capitalistic practices of the time. (Grisar, *Luther*, Freiburg, 1911, III, 472 ff.) That the approach of moral vilification is still considered proper by some scholars is shown again by Jacques Maritain in his book, *Three Reformers*, London, 1928, where portraits of Luther are used to show how he degenerated from a fairly attractive monk to the "bestial" reformer on the deathbed. Maritain says, "The last of the portraits is astoundingly bestial." (p. 168) This type of argument speaks for itself. On the other hand, it is significant that Roman Catholic theologians in Germany have recently developed a far more positive appreciation of Luther and the Reformation, e.g., Joseph Lortz, *Die Reformation in Deutschland*, 2 vols., Freiburg, 1949.

[2] While Roman Catholic critics accuse Luther of being the inspiration of modernism in all its forms (see above), Marxist critics see in him a tool of reaction. As in his own time, Luther

Historical events complicated matters further. Germany, a country influenced strongly by Luther's thought, became a stronghold of totalitarianism, and some liberals were soon discovering in Luther the cause for this development.[3]

However, these critics have never explained why a similar "fascist" development has not taken place in the much more solidly and genuinely Lutheran countries of the North (Sweden, Denmark, Norway, Finland), and have ignored completely the creative influence of Austria and Bavaria

. . . .

is again attacked from the right and from the left simultaneously. Kautsky denounces Luther as a man who denied the lower classes the benefits of the Reformation and always favored the princes. (Karl Kautsky: *Communism in Central Europe in the Time of the Reformation,* London, 1897, p. 128.) In the eyes of modern Marxists, Luther is a child of the dark ages, who hampered progress and burdened the Reformation with a lot of medieval dogmas. According to Hermann Barge, Luther often was a tool of the Catholic reaction, even if not always fully aware of that fact. He allied himself with the established authorities to suppress the proletariat. He destroyed the right of religious self-determination and denied all moral influence upon public life. (Cf. Barge, *Andreas Bodenstein von Karlstadt,* 2 vols., Leipzig, 1905, pp. 439, 451, 460.)

[3] Cf. William McGovern: *From Luther to Hitler* (The History of the Fascist-Nazi Political Philosophy), Boston, 1941. Here Luther is pictured as one of the predecessors of Fascism and Nazism, and the originator of the idea of the national state. The author assumes blithely that from the fifth to the fifteenth century it was generally believed that the pope was and should be the supreme arbiter of all Christians. He assumes that "the pope was held to have ultimate control over the temporal rulers themselves," never mentioning that this was "held" by the pope and his apologists, but not by the temporal rulers. On the whole, this book, like most attempts on the part of liberals to connect Nazism with the Reformation, is distinguished only by its utter disregard of historical facts (see below the discussion of the origin of nationalism). The most flagrant misuse of Luther for the purpose of a Vansittart-Morgenthau plan for Germany can

(solidly Roman Catholic) in the shaping of the National Socialist ideology (not to mention Italy, Spain, and Portugal). In their efforts to connect Luther and Nazism, the liberals were heartily endorsed by Hitler's followers, who tried to claim Luther for themselves. Some, if they were nominally Christian, attempted to use Luther's social ethics to justify their acceptance of Nazism.[4]

Others, if they had openly renounced Christianity, tried to prove that Luther had preceded them and in his own

· ·

be found in Peter F. Wiener, *Martin Luther, Hitler's Spiritual Ancestor,* London, 1945. In a reply to this piece, Gordon Rupp has said: "I hope Mr. Wiener's advisors feel proud to be associated with such methods as he has used. To the rest of us it seems rather sad to think we must win the peace by reviving in England the propaganda devices of the late but unlamented Joseph Goebbels." (*Martin Luther: Hitler's Cause or Cure,* London, 1945.)

[4] Cf. the entire "Schoepfungs-ordnung" school under the leadership of Gogarten and Althaus, e.g., *An Outline of Ethics,* Paul Althaus, translated by A. B. Little, S.T.D. dissertation, Chicago Lutheran Theological Seminary, 1948, p. 193: "Every nation has therefore a twofold task: It is obliged to preserve its biological health and purity and to combat the danger of neglecting its biological duties (racial hygiene). It is to realize its destiny in the individuality and in the special mission that is entrusted to it and to maintain its integrity by warding off all foreign control. It must use every resource at its disposal to execute the creator's plan (i.e., its destiny as a nation) which is latent in its historical situation. This implies for all its members responsibility for the biological maintenance of the nation by means of healthy and qualified posterity. It also implies the duty of loyalty toward the character and fellowship of the nation from which its own life grows. This duty of loyalty which is rooted in love for one's own nation is by no means limited simply to the state boundary but under certain conditions also to extraordinary circumstances (men 'between the nations') or to gigantic historical tasks, even to the emigration and resettlement of nations (as, e.g., America)." Althaus is considered a leader in

thought "transcended" Christianity.[5]

The pseudo-historians of Nazism and of liberalism agreed that National Socialism was the logical conclusion of the Reformation. The confusion was further increased by the fact that there were some Roman Catholic scholars who studied Luther's social ethics and found him in basic agreement with Thomas Aquinas. They asserted, with the endorsement of the Roman Catholic bishops and the *Censor Librorum,* that on the basis of the notion of natural law, Catholics and Lutherans could be good Nazis.[6]

Of course, there are also the professional Luther scholars, but even if they have loudly disagreed with all other views, each one has had a different interpretation of Luther's social ethics.[7] As a result, even some of them have given

. . . .

the so-called "neo-Lutheran" movement. Cf. also Werner Betcke, *Luthers Sozialethik,* Gütersloh, 1934, where the introduction is used to show how timely Luther's thought is and how nicely he fits in with the (Nazi) reformation of the German state.

[5] Cf. Arno Deutelmoser, *Luther, Staat, und Glaube,* Jena, 1937. Here the author tries to show that Luther's concept of the hidden God (*deus absconditus*) whose power is at work in everything makes a Christian distinction between good and evil impossible. He says (pp. 50 ff.), "Luther overcomes Christianity from within."

[6] See Franz Xavier Arnold, *Zur Frage des Naturrechts bei Martin Luther,* Munich, 1937, Imprimatur Bishop of Rothenburg. The author attempts to find a common ground upon which Roman Catholics and Lutherans alike can justify their agreement with the Nazi state (p. vi).

[7] The most important controversy was that between Ernst Troeltsch and Karl Holl. In his *Social Teachings of the Christian Churches,* New York, 1931, Troeltsch emphasized the unresolved dichotomy between personal and official morality in Luther. The personal demands of Christian ethics are contrasted with the social demands of natural law, which results, according to Troeltsch, in two different moral standards for the Christian

up every attempt to find in Luther a consistent view.[8]

It is small wonder that under these circumstances R. H. Tawney, after surveying the field, threw up his hands and said, "Luther's utterances on social morality are the occasional explosions of a capricious volcano, with only a rare flash of light amid the torrent of smoke and flame, and it is idle to scan them for a coherent and consistent doctrine. Compared with the lucid and subtle rationalism of a thinker like St. Antonio, his sermons and pamphlets on social questions make an impression of naïvete, as of an impetuous but ill-informed genius, dispensing with the cumbrous embarrassments of law and logic, to evolve a system of social ethics from the inspired heat of his own unsophisticated consciousness."[9] If Tawney were right, then every effort to

. . . .

who follows Luther (pp. 501, 509, 532).

Against this view Karl Holl (*Gesammelte Aufsätze zur Kirchengeschichte,* Tübingen, 1923, I, *Luther,* 243), asserts, "Luther has no recourse to natural law. . . ." and he continues, "As far as Luther is concerned, the confusion which dominates Troeltsch is solved as soon as it is recognized that the notion of *lex naturae,* as usually used by Max Weber and Troeltsch, has merely been injected into Luther from the outside."

[8] According to Walther Köhler, *Luther und das Luthertum in ihrer weltgeschichtlichen Auswirkung,* Leipzig, 1903, Luther had no solution to the problem of the Christian in the world. He says: "The entire legitimation of the secular realm (*weltlich Ding*) as a divine order is and remains for Luther an emergency measure, necessary because we must live in this world. But just this fact was not taken into consideration by the early Christians. And Luther does not subordinate this world to the Christian theological coercion. He is too much of an 'early Christian' to do that. As he sees it, the sharpest tension exists between Christianity and the world. But this is no solution to the problem, as far as I can see. On the contrary, everything remains in a state of suspension." (p. 134, note to p. 130)

[9] R. H. Tawney, *Religion and the Rise of Capitalism,* New York, 1926, pp. 79 ff.

21

speak of Luther's social ethics would be doomed from the start. In that case, an analysis of Luther's social ethics would consist of collecting inconsistent and illogical utterances. Yet at the same time, and from a very pragmatic point of view, it would leave unexplained the actual social development in those countries where Luther's theological views were accepted. It would take away the historical motivation for the peculiar development in the realm of social ethics in the countries dominated by the Lutheran Reformation. It is relatively easy to say about Luther: "Confronted with the complexities of foreign trade and financial organization, or with the subtleties of economic analysis, he is like a savage introduced to a dynamo or a steam engine."[10] The only difficulty with such an interpretation is that it leaves unexplained the tremendous influence of this sociological savage. There must be some explanation for Gustavus Adolphus of Sweden, Grundtvig and the Folkschool and cooperative movements in Denmark, and the social legislation which so clearly distinguishes countries which have been under the influence of Lutheran ethics from those under the influence of Roman Catholic or Calvinistic ethics. It may be that Luther's social concern was understood more clearly by some of his followers than it was understood by his critics. In that case, Luther must have had a social ethics, of which the principles, at least, were understandable to those who came under the influence of his views. The main reason for an investigation into Luther's social ethics cannot be the present

. . . .

[10] Ibid., p. 89.

[11] See the interesting application of the principles from an utterly practical point of view in A. T. Jorgensen, *Filantropi,* Copenhagen, 1939. See also Martin von Nathusius, *Die Mitarbeit der Kirche an der Lösung der Sozialen Frage,* Leipzig, 1904.

[12] John Calvin, *Institutes of the Christian Religion,* trans. John Allen, Philadelphia, 1936, II, 780.

[13] That Calvinistic biblicism applied to the social realm can

state of Luther research. Here utter confusion seems to rule and would indicate the futility of any such undertaking. But if Luther's social ethics is considered in terms of the motivation which it may have supplied to "Lutherans," then the investigation becomes more rewarding.[11]

It seems that wherever Lutheranism has been the dominant religious force it has contributed to a view of society and its "orders" which is basically different from other prevalent concepts. This difference can be illustrated by using the notion of the "state." Here Lutheranism has contributed to a view which, for better or for worse, is clearly distinguishable from the views of other religious forces that have influenced society. Roman Catholicism creates a state which at its best is the secular instrument of the church as a hierarchical institution. In practice it creates states like present-day Spain, Portugal, Argentina, or 1934-38 Austria. Calvinism creates a state where God should rule through magistrates who will be expected to establish the pure worship of God according to His law, and "employ their uttermost efforts in asserting and defending the honor of Him whose vice-regents they are and by whose favor they govern."[12] This creates the puritanical theocracy of Geneva, Scotland, and New England, and is today found in certain small United States communities.[13]

The other-worldliness of the sect (the *Schwaermer* and the Anabaptist movement with all their modern representatives) considers the state the enemy of the people and the realm of

. . . .

have most unfortunate consequences has been seen in South Africa—and to a certain extent in the South of the United States —where the most orthodox Calvinists have often proved to be the most fanatical racists. Cf. Arnold Toynbee, *A Study of History,* London, 1935, I, 211: "The 'Bible Christian' of European origin and race who has settled among peoples of non-European race overseas, has inevitably identified himself with Israel obeying the will of Jehovah and doing the Lord's work by taking possession of the promised land, while he has identified the devil. This concept, which has influenced old-line political liberalism, merely tolerates the state as a necessary evil. According to this view, the only excuse for the existence of the state seems to be that from the point of view of the all-important individual the state is useful. Here we find the admiration for that state which has no positive or creative function and is merely dedicated to the proposition of maintaining law and order in the most superficial and formal manner. Here politics is considered by nature "dirty," and no respectable Christian should get involved in it.[14]

Lutheranism, on the other hand, has created a view of the state as a divine order endowed by God with certain creative tasks and quite independent from the church as an ecclesiastical institution. The peculiar responsibility which the state has to protect and secure the welfare of its citizens is illustrated in the Scandinavian countries. The very fact that here the state as state—and not under the direct control of the organized church—takes an active part in promoting the general welfare of the citizens, is a typical expression of this concept of the state as a creative organism with specific divine tasks, quite independent from the tasks of the organized church. Here the influence of the church upon the state can be exerted only personally, through the "communion of

. . . .

the non-Europeans who have crossed his path with the Canaanites whom the Lord has delivered into the hands of his chosen people to be destroyed or subjugated."

[14] It is important to note that this "sect" point of view is common to all other-worldly groups, even to the sects within the other churches. This applies to certain religious orders

24

saints," not institutionally as in Roman Catholicism or legally as in Calvinism. Nevertheless, and in opposition to the sect and pietism, the state is not merely a necessary evil, but a divine gift in which the Christian has to take his responsibilities with everybody else.[15]

Besides these religiously conditioned concepts of the state, there are, of course, those contemporary concepts which have been inspired by secular ideologies. Totalitarian Fascism and National Socialism find their inspiration in romantic naturalism, while totalitarian Marxism is inspired by materialistic naturalism, Hegelian pantheism standing godfather to both.

If the various concepts of the state are related to ideological antecedents, as claimed above, we should be able to find a similar relationship in the case of other orders of society, such as the family and vocation. If there is evidence that an independent view of society and its task and standards developed on Lutheran soil, we may ask whether there is any indication that Luther's thought is responsible for such a development. However, before such a study of Luther's social ethics can be undertaken, a number of difficulties must be discussed and, if possible, removed.

. . . .

within Roman Catholicism and the great stream of pietism within Lutheranism and Calvinism, and adds considerable confusion to the picture.

[15] See the very illuminating discussion of Luther's concept of "Calling" in Einar Billing, *Our Calling,* (1909), translated from the Swedish by Conrad Bergendoff, Rock Island, Illinois, 1947.

III. THE DIFFICULTIES

Before an evaluation of Luther's social ethics is possible, a number of important sociological developments that have been commonly attributed to Luther and the Reformation must be examined and their relevance to our investigation ascertained.

Too much has been made of the influence of Luther and the Reformation in general upon the development of capitalism and nationalism. The far-reaching results of these forces cannot be denied. They, more than anything else, have shaped the world of modern man. But in spite of all claims from enemies and friends of the Reformation, it does not seem possible to describe them as results of the Reformation.[1] When a recent standard textbook states that the Reformation "ultimately sanctioned a newly capitalistic, nationalistic and individualistic world,"[2] it seems that many of the creative movements of the outgoing Middle Ages have been badly confused and that history has been forced into a pre-conceived pattern which must prove a strait jacket to historical veracity.[3] Every perusal of the sources will show that capitalism existed and blossomed before Luther ever entered the picture.[4] To be sure, it was a monopoly capitalism of the papacy, the princes, and a few great banking

. . . .

[1] The famous investigations of Max Weber, *Gesammelte Aufsätze Zur Religionssoziologie,* Tübingen, 1922, and Troeltsch, *Social Teachings,* have asserted primarily that Calvinism had a particular affinity to capitalism and was responsible for its growth. Although this thesis is questionable even within this limited framework, it is quite indefensible when applied by the popularizers to the Reformation as a whole.

[2] *Introduction to Contemporary Civilization in the West,* a source book prepared by the Contemporary Civilization staff of Columbia College, Columbia University, New York, 1947, I, 468.

houses, but it was capitalism nevertheless. Capitalism did not start at Wittenberg or Geneva, but if a place of birth has to be found, Rome would be the most likely choice. The peculiar revenue system of the papacy, which reached all over Europe, could not work efficiently within a feudal or land society. The world-wide financial demands of the Holy See made some form of money economy a necessity. The political ambitions of the papacy had resulted in perpetual financial difficulties. These difficulties could be solved only by means of steadily increasing loans.[5] This development had begun as early as Pope Alexander III (1159-1181).

In order to be able to repay these loans and to supply the steadily increasing financial needs of the papacy, all types of new taxes were devised, and with them a machinery for collection. Within this machinery bankers soon began to play a most important part. Early in the fifteenth century, the money which the papacy collected was deposited with some representative of a banking house, and often the Medici were chosen.[6]

Soon the papacy used the established banking houses as its agents and became thoroughly involved in the rising capitalistic system: "When the rising Italian capitalists began to establish agencies in the various commercial centers of Europe, they offered better facilities for the growing fiscal business of the papacy. By the time of Pope Gregory IX

. . . .

[3] Cf. Lujo Brentano, *Die Anfaenge des modernen Kapitalismus,* Munich, 1916; H. M. Robertson, *The Rise of Economic Individualism,* Cambridge, 1933; and Tawney, op. cit.

[4] To the following cf. William Lunt, *Papal Revenues in the Middle Ages,* New York, 1934.

[5] F. Schneider, "Zur älteren päpstlichen Finanzgeschichte," *Quellen und Forschungen aus italienischen Bibliotheken,* IX, 2, as quoted in Tawney.

[6] Lunt, I, 19.

(1227-1241), Italian merchants had become the principal bankers of the camera."[7] There can be no doubt that the patronage of the papacy helped these Italian bankers greatly in the development of the capitalistic machinery. Since the papacy itself often paid interest on its loans, [8] one can safely say that the medieval popes not only sanctioned but through their fiscal policy helped create modern capitalism. Although Dante considered the Cahorsine moneylenders fit only for hell—and put them there—Innocent IV gave them in 1248 the title of "special sons of the Roman Church."[9] In view of the close association of interests and of families (the same Italian noble families dominated the religious and the secular life), it is not surprising to find that the banking interests enjoyed the special protection of the papacy[10] and that the Roman Church not only encouraged the capitalistic development[11] but was involved in lending money at interest.[12] Since the facts are so evident and abundant that capitalism came into existence and flourished with the sanction of the papacy long before the Protestant Reformation,

. . . .

[7] Ibid., p. 51.

[8] The following excerpt from the Vatican Archives, translated in Lunt, I, 316, should demonstrate beyond a doubt that the Reformation was not needed to sanction capitalism: "Item, there were paid by the lord of Camerarius to the lord legate in Parma, for the month of the aforesaid June, for certain merchants of Parma, for interest (usura) on 1200 gold florins, received as a loan from those merchants by that lord Camerarius and sent by him to Borgo San Connino for making the advance or stipendiary payments of the church existing there, 28 gold florins and 20 imperial shillings . . . at the rate of 2 florins and 12s 4d imperial for the hundred each month." (A rate of interest of about $2\frac{1}{2}\%$ per month, or 30% annually!)

[9] R. Ehrenberg, Das Zeitalter der Fugger, Jena, 1895, II, 66.

[10] Matthew Paris, Chronica Majora, V, 404-405 as quoted in Tawney, p. 294, note 29.

[11] For specific documentation see Tawney, p. 294, note 31,

the assertion that it was the Reformation and Luther which caused the rise of capitalism seems absurd.

The Lutheran Reformation, far from sanctioning the new capitalistic society, contained a strong element of revolt against the exploitation of the people by the capitalistic practices of the papacy. It is worthy of note that the pope who clashed with Luther was a Medici banker and that the indulgence salesmen were always accompanied by a representative of the Fugger banking house. The bankers had a great stake in the collection of the indulgence money, since they had advanced the funds to Albrecht of Hohenzollern which had enabled him to purchase his three ecclesiastical offices and the necessary papal dispensation.[13] Though strong statements against usury can be found in the works of the scholastic theologians, the effect of these "blue laws" in the late Middle Ages was negligible. Encouraged by the actual practice of the papacy—which sometimes used the threat of excommunication to compel men to pay the usurious interests demanded by Italian moneylenders—[14]

. . . .

and 300-01, note 88. See also Hermann Barge, *Luther und der Frühkapitalismus,* Gütersloh, 1951, pp. 7 ff.

[12] Achille Luchaire, *Social France at the Time of Philip Augustus,* trans. Edward B. Krehbiel, New York, 1912; see Tawney, p. 294, note 32. The chapter of Notre Dame in Paris lent money at interest to those who were in need of it.

[13] See Aloys Schulte, *Die Fugger in Rom, 1495-1523,* 2 vols., Leipzig, 1904. The following Papal acquittance is translated and reprinted in Lunt, II, 485: "March 23, 1512, Pope Julius II: Of our motion, etc., we acknowledge by the present to have received in ready and counted cash from the beloved sons Jacob Fugger and relatives (nepotibus), German merchant following the Roman court, the sum of 6027 ¾ in gold ducats of the camera, which money, as that Jacob and relatives say that they had notice of the month of last January which came from the city of Augsburg, had been exacted in the Kingdom of Poland and in the territory of Breslau of Silesia from the jubilee granted in that kingdom. . . ."

and the spirit of the age, the power and influence of capitalism increased steadily before the Reformation ever began.[15] Four hundred years before Luther complained about the financial abuses of the papacy, St. Bernard had exclaimed about the church, which he loved: "Wealth is drawn up by ropes of wealth thus money bringeth money. . . . O vanity of vanities, yet no more vain than insane! The Church is resplendent in her walls, beggarly in her poor. She clothes her stones in gold, and leaves her sons naked."[16]

Luther, unlike the banker-theologians who opposed him and whose spokesman, John Eck, had defended usury in a public disputation at Bologna, had a deep and simple dislike for usury and the sharp business practices which he noted all about him. As early as 1519, he had published a tract opposing usury. He repeated his accusations in 1520 in his *Open Letter to the Christian Nobility*. Here he said, "We must put a bit in the mouth of the Fuggers and similar corporations. How is it possible that in the lifetime of a single man such great possessions, worthy of a king, can be piled up, and yet everything be done legally and according to God's will? I am not a mathematician, but I do not understand how a man with a hundred gulden can make a profit of twenty gulden in one year, nay, how with one gulden he can make another; and that, too, by another way than agri-

. . . .

[14] Cf. Tawney, p. 29.
[15] Ibid., p. 29, "The Papacy was, in a sense, the greatest financial institution of the Middle Ages, and, as its fiscal system was elaborated, things became not better but worse. The abuses which were a trickle in the thirteenth century were a torrent in the fifteenth. And the frailties of Rome, if exceptional in their notoriety, can hardly be regarded as unique. Priests, it is from time to time complained, engage in trade and take usury. Cathedral chapters lend money at high rates of interest. The profits of usury, like those of simony, should have been refused by churchmen as hateful to God; but a bishop of Paris, when consulted by a usurer as to the salvation of his soul, instead of urging restitution, recommended him to dedicate his ill-gotten

30

culture or cattle-raising, in which increase of wealth depends not on human wits, but on God's blessing." In the same year he dealt with the subject again in his *Treatise on Usury,* and in 1524 he wrote another tract, *On Trading and Usury.* All reveal Luther's sincere revulsion against capitalism and all its works and an almost pathetic nostalgia for a less commercial age. "This I know well," he says, "that it would be much more pleasing to God if we increased agriculture and diminished commerce."[17] In view of these clearly and abundantly expressed views, it is difficult to defend the view that Luther encouraged the development of a "capitalistic world."

Another of the great society-forming forces whose origin has been attributed to Luther and the Reformation is nationalism. It has been said, "The very notion of the national state emerged into public consciousness only after and largely as a result of the Reformation."[18] And not only modern nationalism but especially the totalitarian form of nationalism is supposed to be a direct result of Luther's theory of the state. It has thus been said, "The historical result of the original motives and the early history of the Reformation was an uncompromising, realistic and entirely amoral authoritarianism."[19] The examples of similar opinions, expressed more or less vociferously, could be multi-

. . . .

wealth to the building of Notre Dame."

[16] From a letter of St. Bernard, c. 1125, quoted in Tawney, p. 30. If the Reformation (particularly in its Calvinistic mode) had an influence upon capitalism, it was the tendency to democratize it. From the capitalism of the few—clergy, princes and bankers—it became the capitalism of the many. Under Calvinistic auspices everybody has a chance to be a capitalist.

[17] Phila. Ed., II, 160 ff. (Open Letter to the Christian Nobility). See also Ibid., IV, 9-69 (On Trading and Usury and Treatise on Usury).

[18] McGovern, p. 21.

[19] Eduard Heimann, *Freedom and Order,* New York, 1947, p.

plied.[20] But for an investigation of Luther's social ethics it is of the greatest importance to discover whether Luther can justly be called the creator—even if only accidentally— of the modern national state.

That such a claim cannot be made for Luther without virtually suppressing the history of the entire medieval period, should be clear to even the most superficial observer. The national state is the result of the conflict between the two universal powers which dominate the Middle Ages, the emperor and the pope. Far from being an idyllic period of universal peace and Christian virtue, the Middle Ages were a period of intense conflict between ambitious emperors (e.g., Hohenstauffen) and equally ambitious popes (e.g., Gregory VII, Alexander III, Innocent III, Innocent IV).[21]

. . . .

46. Cf. p. 42: "(Lutheran doctrine) includes the two propositions that the authority is entitled to our unqualified loyalty, and— even more striking—that the political decisions to be made by the authority are essentially exempt from moral judgment."

[20] Cf. Wiener, *Martin Luther, Hitler's Spiritual Ancestor,* popular article by Dean William R. Inge, as quoted in *Time,* Nov. 6, 1944; and others.

[21] Cf. the following description of the conflict in the *Monumenta Germaniae Historia,* ed. Georg Heinrich Pertz, XIX, 342, as quoted in Toynbee, IV, 563-64: "In those days wickedness prevailed; the people of God were without a ruler; Rome lay desolate; the glory of the clergy departed; and the people of God were divided. Some followed the Church, and these took the Cross (against Frederick), while others followed Frederick the cidevant Emperor, and these insulted the Divine Religion . . . Mercy and Truth and Justice were no longer to be found on Earth."

[22] For the immediate results see Salimbene's *Chronicle,* Parma, 1857, pp. 70-71, as quoted in Toynbee, IV, 564-565, where we find this description of the medieval "utopia," the period of absolute papal power: "Men could neither plough nor sow nor reap nor cultivate the vine nor gather the vintage nor live on

In this conflict the emperor represented the more "democratic" power since he was a feudal lord, dependent upon the good will of his vassals. The emperor did not inherit his office but was elected to it. The papacy, on the other hand, asserted since Hildebrand (1073-1085) claims of an absolute right to rule the world. The ambitions of these two great powers had to clash violently, and the history of the Middle Ages is the record of this conflict. Since the papacy did not hesitate to use physical force to attain spiritual ends (the notion of the "crusade" is typical of the papacy, medieval and modern), these secular means showed a tendency to become ends in themselves. This had the most catastrophic consequences for Christendom, for Europe, and ultimately for the papacy itself.[22] Hildebrand, who had begun his

. . . .

the farms—especially in the territories of Parma, Reggio, Modena, and Cremona. Close to the cities themselves, however, men tilled the ground under the guard of the city militia, who were divided into quarters corresponding to the city gates. Armed soldiers guarded the laborers all day, and the country people carried on their agricultural work under these conditions. This was necessary on account of the highwaymen, thieves and robbers who had multiplied exceedingly and who kidnapped people and carried them off to dungeons to be ransomed for money. They also lifted the cattle and ate or sold them. If their prisoners did not raise a ransom they hanged them by the feet or hands and pulled out their teeth and put paddocks and toads in their mouths to hurry them up in producing the ransom money; and these tortures were more bitter and abominable to them than any form of death. The brigands were more cruel than demons; and in those times one human being was about as glad to meet another human being on the road as he would have been to meet the Devil himself; for everyone was living in perpetual suspicion of everyone else—suspecting his neighbor of intending to kidnap him and throw him into a dungeon, in order that 'the ransom of a man's life might be his riches' (Proverbs 13:8). So the land was reduced to desert, empty of both husbandman and wayfarer. For in the days of Frederick—and especially after his deposition from the Imperial office, and after Parma had ecclesiastical career as "cappelanus" to Gregory VI, by raising a small army to fight the local Roman gangster-noblemen who were stealing the money from the altar of the pope's own church, died in exile at Salerno, while Rome was being looted by the Normans called by Hildebrand to help him fight his political battles when he had acceded to the papacy.[23] This episode is typical for the medieval papacy. Like Goethe's sorcerer's apprentice, they were calling upon spirits which they could not control. In the struggle against the universal power of the empire, the popes had to rely upon the national and parochial powers of the kings and princes. In order to weaken the emperor, they had to strengthen the much more autocratic and absolute national princes.[24] This policy brought temporary success. The papacy triumphed over the empire and Europe's central authority was so weakened that it became a pawn in the hands of pope and princes. But it soon proved an empty victory as far as the papacy was concerned. The spoils went to the princes who had supported the pope in his struggle. The pope, who had taught the princes how to collect money for his war against the emperor, had to sit idly by, once the machinery had been established, while kings and princes pocketed the revenues collected for the purposes of the papacy.[25] Eventually, instead of being plagued by one strong emperor, the papacy was now surrounded by a strong

. . . .

rebelled against him and lifted her heel—'the highways were unoccupied, and the travelers walked through byways' (Judges 5:6) and evils multiplied on the earth. Wild birds and wild animals multiplied quite beyond measure—pheasants, partridges and quails, hares, roebuck, and fallow-deer, buffaloes, wild boars and ravening wolves. These wild beasts no longer found creatures —lambs or sheep—to eat, as they had been used to finding them, on the farms, because the farms had been burnt to ashes. And so the wolves used to gather in packs round the moat of a city to howl aloud under the extreme torment of their hunger. And they used to creep into the cities by night and devour people— women and children among them—who were sleeping under

France, England, and Spain. The powerful national states of Louis XI in France, of Ferdinand and Isabella in Spain, and of Henry VII in England were the spirits which the papacy had called and now had no power to dismiss or dominate.

When Boniface VIII tried to oppose the king of France in the manner in which his predecessors had opposed the emperor, he soon learned that a new age had dawned. The new national states proved impregnable against the papal wrath, and the pope soon found himself the virtual prisoner of the French king. As in a tremendous card game, the papacy had overplayed its hand, and when the bluff was called its inner weakness was revealed.

The "Babylonian Captivity" of the papacy (1309-1376) was followed by the "Great Schism" (1378-1417). In its gamble for political power the papacy had lost. The victor in the struggle for power between pope and emperor was nationalism, and this victory, established long before the Reformation, had its source in the political ambitions of the papacy:

> "The position of unrivaled dominance in Western Christendom, to which the papacy finally attained through its victory in its war to the knife with the Hohenstaufen Dynasty, of course placed on the papacy's shoulders a unique responsibility for worthily and successfully upholding the oecu-

. . . .

porches or in wagons. Sometimes they even burrowed through the house walls and strangled the babies in their cradles. No one who had not seen them—as I saw them—could believe the horrors which were committed at that time, not only by men, but by beasts of various kinds."

[23] Cf. Toynbee, IV, 536 ff. See also *Cambridge Medieval History,* New York, 1924-36, V, 51 ff.

[24] For Luther's attitude towards that medieval controversy, see W.A., 54, 300 ff. (Papsttreu Hadriani IV Und Alexander III, 1545.)

[25] Cf. Toynbee, IV, 534-35, 539-40.

menical principle of which it had deliberately made itself the exclusive exponent when it insisted upon delivering a 'knockout blow' to its already discomfited adversary, the Holy Roman Empire. In so far as it failed to live up to this self-imposed responsibility, the papacy was in part the cause of the subsequent outbreak of Parochialism, of which it was also the most eminent victim; and its share of bringing the new spirit of Parochialism to a head was undoubtedly very large. The 'hybris' with which the papacy exploited its victory over the Empire—in first trampling on a prostrate foe and then attempting to exercise on its own account the oecumenical despotism which it had refused to tolerate in the hands of a Barbarossa or a Frederick II—quickly turned the public opinion of Western Christendom, not only against the papacy itself, but against the whole principle of oecumenicalism which was now embodied in the papacy alone."[26]

But before the ultimate triumph of the particular over the universal and of the autocratic over the "democratic" forces, Europe and Christendom received one more opportunity to solve their problems in a corporate and almost "democratic" manner. And here again it was the papacy which failed

. . . .

[26] Toynbee, IV, 215, note 1.

[27] Toynbee, following A. H. Thompson, points out (IV, 562) that it was during this struggle that a pope (Innocent III) whose predecessors had called themselves "Vicar of Peter" suddenly adopted the title "Vicar of Christ." See also *Cambridge Medieval History,* VI, 644: "Soon after he ascended the papal throne, Innocent III began to use the phrase 'Vicar of Christ' in connection with his office. It had not been used before his time; and the implication that the successors of Peter were not his deputies, but received their commission as he did, immediately from Christ, is significant of the conviction upon which the policy of Innocent was founded. . . . The assertions of Innocent III went

Christendom. It was the Conciliar Movement of the fifteenth century which presented Europe with its last opportunity to settle its problems in a universal and constitutional manner. Had the papacy been able to learn from the past, this movement might have succeeded. But the popes, whose pride had grown beyond all measure during their successful struggle with the empire[27] and for whom pride was the only means of support during the "Babylonian Captivity" and the "Great Schism," were unable to learn anything from history.[28] Thus, they frustrated every effort on the part of the councils to bring about a genuine reformation of the church by denying the very right of a council to reform the papacy. Yet the conciliar movement presented the possibility of reuniting the centrifugal forces of the age within the framework of a political federation under Christian auspices. Within this federation the papacy could have obtained a "limited constitutional authority over a loyal and undivided Christian Commonwealth,"[29] but instead the pope (Martin V) elected by the Council of Constance confirmed, after his election, the rules of the papal chancery promulgated under John XXIII, a "Vicar of Christ" who was accused of piracy, murder, rape, sodomy, and incest by the same council.[30] For the sake of papal solidarity Martin gave up the idea of reforming the papacy. As a result, the popes that followed after the Council of Constance, among them the notorious

. . . .

far to establish the Papacy in the possession of semi-divine honours."

[28] In his bull, "Execrabilis" (1459), Pius II (Enea Silvio Piccolomini) condemned any appeal to a general council as heresy and "lèse-majesté." Carl Mirbt, *Quellen zur Geschichte des Papsttums und des Römischen Katholizismus,* 3rd ed., Tübingen, 1911, p. 181. See also John T. McNeill, *Unitive Protestantism,* Nashville, 1930, pp. 89 ff.

[29] Toynbee, IV, 573.

[30] See Edward Gibbon, *The History of the Decline and Fall of the Roman Empire,* New York, 1900, VI, 612.

Alexander VI, were even worse than those who had come before.

This situation was not altered by the abortive attempts for reform by the Council of Basel (1431-49) which the pope undermined with a "counter-council" at Florence.[31] The Conciliar Movement failed because of the opposition of the papacy, and thus the papacy itself contributed more than any other power to the disintegration of Western Christendom into the small absolute kingdoms that characterize the modern development.

For our investigation, however, it is of the greatest importance to note that the conciliar struggle for constitutional unity within Christendom, which was so vehemently opposed by the papacy, was wholeheartedly endorsed by

. . . .

[31] Ibid. VI, 407 ff.

[32] Luther's "conciliarism" has been clearly pointed out by John T. McNeill, pp. 96-109: "But with Luther and his adherents conciliarism was much more than a traditional theory. In crisis after crisis they made vigorous demands and appeals for a free general council. For many years after the controversy began they hopefully looked forward to its settlement by conciliar action." (p. 99) This is a much-neglected aspect of Luther's political theory.

[33] W.A., 6, 404 ff. Cf. Phila. Ed., II, 77: "They [the spokesmen for the papacy and especially Prierias] have no basis in Scripture for their contention that it belongs to the pope alone to call a council or confirm its actions; for this is based merely upon their own laws, which are valid only insofar as they are not injurious to Christendom or contrary to the laws of God. When the pope deserves punishment, such laws go out of force, since it is injurious to Christendom not to punish by means of a council. Thus we read in Acts XV that it was not St. Peter who called the Apostolic Council, but the Apostles and Elders. If, then, that right had belonged to St. Peter alone, the council would not have been a Christian Council, but a heretical conciliabulum. Even the Council of Nicea—the most famous of all—was neither called nor confirmed by the Bishop of Rome but by the Emperor

38

Luther and the Reformation.[32] From 1520, when Luther asked for a council in order to bring about the reformation of church and society in his famous *Open Letter To The Christian Nobility*,[33] to the very end of his life, he hoped for the settlement of the difficulties which confronted Christendom through a general council.[34] Luther rejoiced when Charles V was elected German emperor, not for nationalistic reasons, for Charles was a foreigner, but because he hoped that this "noble young blood" would have the ability and the power to bring about a reformation of church and society.[35] It was the pope who tried to bring about the election of an impotent German prince in order to postpone indefinitely any reformation of the Curia.[36] And it was the papacy whose tireless political maneuvers further decimated

. . . .

Constantine. . . . Therefore, when necessity demands, and the pope is an offence to Christendom, the first man who is able should, as a faithful member of the whole body, do what he can to bring about a truly free council."

[34] During his lectures on Genesis, which occupied the last years of his life (1535-1545; cf. W.A., 42, vii), he commented on the reluctance of the Evangelicals at Smalcald to attend a papal council with the following words: "Thus it happened when we were at Smalcald and rejected the pope and his council. But it would have been far better had we not turned it down if only it could have been conducted fairly." (W.A., 43, 116, 7)

[35] W.A., 6, 405, 20; cf. Phila. Ed., II, 63: "Ofttimes the councils have made some pretence at reformation, but their attempts have been cleverly hindered by the guile of certain men and things have gone from bad to worse. I now intend, by the help of God, to throw some light upon the wiles and wickedness of these men, to the end that when they are known, they may not henceforth be so hurtful and so great a hindrance. God has given us a noble youth to be our head and thereby awakened great hopes of good in many hearts, wherefore it is meet that we should do our part and profitably use this time of grace."

[36] Cf. Heinrich Boehmer, *Road to Reformation*, Philadelphia, 1946, pp. 258 ff.

the unity of Western Christendom, placing Florentine and Medici self-interest above the welfare of the Christian body politic.[37] While the Lutherans continuously pressed for a free and general council, the papacy used every means to prevent the emperor from bringing it about.[38]

Only toward the end of his life did Luther realize that a council would not be held unless the pope could control the outcome beforehand. He felt that under such circumstances any genuine reformation of the Roman church could not be

. . . .

[37] L. v. Ranke, *History of the Popes,* London, 1852, pp. 23 ff. How little Clement VII (Guilo de Medici, of the same Florentine banking family as Leo X) cared about Christian unity is shown by his attitude towards Charles V during the Diet of Speier (1526). Cf. Ranke, p. 29: "In the summer of 1526, we see the Italians at last going to work with their own strength. The Milanese are already in the field against the Imperialists. A Venetian and papal army advance to their support. Swiss aid is promised and the alliance of France and England has been secured. 'This time,' said Giberto, the most confidential minister of Clement VII, 'the matter concerns not a petty revenge, a point of honour, or a single town. This war decides the liberation or the perpetual thraldom of Italy.' He expresses no doubt of a successful issue. 'Posterity will envy us that their lot had not been cast on our days, that they might have witnessed so high fortune and have had their part in it.' He hopes there will be no foreign aid. 'Ours alone will be the glory, and so much sweeter the fruit.' With these thoughts and hopes Clement entered on his war against the Spaniards. . . . The pope seemed to have left the commotions of Germany wholly out of considera-tion." The result of this bit of "political realism" on the part of Clement VII was the sack of Rome (May 6, 1527).

[38] Preface to the *Augsburg Confession,* H. E. Jacobs, *Book of Concord,* Philadelphia, 1908, p. 35: "In the event, therefore, that the differences between us and the other parties in the matter of religion cannot be amicably and in charity settled here before Your Imperial Majesty, we offer this in all obedience, abundantly prepared to join issue and to defend the cause in such a general, free, Christian Council, for the convening of

expected. In 1545 he complained, "What good will it do to spend so much money and effort to bring about a council, if the pope decides beforehand what the council can do and that everything should be subject to him and nothing should be done except according to his pleasure, reserving himself the right to condemn everything?"[39] But it was the Curia, not Luther, which had made impossible a constructive solution of the problems raised by the medieval death struggle between papacy and empire.[40]

. . . .

which there has always been accordant action and agreement of votes in all the Imperial Diets held during Your Majesty's reign, on the part of the Electors, Princes, and other Estates of the Empire. To this General Council, and at the same time to Your Imperial Majesty, we have made appeal in this greatest and gravest of matters even before this in due manner and form of law. To this appeal both to Your Imperial Majesty and to a Council, we still adhere; neither do we intend, nor would it be possible for us, to relinquish it by this or any other document." See also *Smalcald Articles*, W.A., 50, 192 ff., and Luther's preface to *Suggestions of A Committee of Cardinals* (1538), W.A., 50, 288, 1 ff. "The pope is carrying this poor council around like a cat her kittens. He doesn't want to hold it in Germany. He claims he cannot hold it in Mantua. Now he has chosen Vicenza where it cannot be held and where they have no intention of holding it. It seems that he is going to become a real Marcolfus who could nowhere find the right tree to hang himself. Thus the pope cannot discover a place where he would like to hold a council." For the attitude of the pope, see also the letter from Paul III to Charles V asserting that the emperor has no business to ask for a council (St. L., XVII, pp. 998-99).

[39] W.A., 54, 206 ff. (Against the Papacy in Rome, 1545).

[40] Toynbee, IV, 576: "After the turn of the fifteenth and sixteenth centuries the power which the papacy had refused to share constitutionally with a parliament of the Christian commonwealth was lawlessly snatched out of its hands by the parochial secular princes, who might have been kept within bounds by the oecumenical authority of a Pope in council, but

In view of these facts it seems impossible to attribute the origin or even the strengthening of nationalism to Luther. Nationalism, or "Parochialism," as Toynbee calls it more accurately,[41] developed long before the Reformation. It developed more effectively on Catholic soil, and reached its peak in the absolutism of a French Catholic Louis XIV rather than a Swedish Lutheran Gustavus Adolphus II.[42] And the "realistic" nationalist politicians of our age, who consider treaties mere "scraps of paper," have more in common with the papacy, which unilaterally dissolved solemn treaties if they became politically burdensome, than

· ·

who now found an easy prey in a Pope who alienated and disillusioned the *plebs Christiana* by recklessly setting his own will to power against the people's yearning for reform and relief."

[41] Modern nationalism is the result of the romantic movement, and the term cannot be meaningfully applied to Prussian kings who speak broken German, e.g., Frederick II, or English kings who speak broken English, e.g., George I.

[42] Ibid., IV, 219: "In the modern Western World, however, Parochial Sovereignty has never been a monopoly of the Protestant countries. One source of it, as we have seen, has been the constellation of Italian city-states which arose before Protestantism was heard of, in a part of Western Christendom in which Protestantism has never gained a footing. And in the Transalpine world at the beginning of the Modern Age, Parochial Sovereignty raised its head in the Protestant and the Catholic countries simultaneously . . . and some of the most high-handedly revolutionary apostles of the 'totalitarian state' —from a Hapsburg Joseph II and a Corsican Napoleon I to a Romagnol Mussolini and an Upper-Austrian Hitler—are the nurslings of purely Catholic environments."

[43] In his *Open Letter to the Christian Nobility,* Luther attacks the pope for his claim to have the right to dissolve solemn political treaties between sovereign powers if they do not meet with his approval. Referring to a treaty between Wladislav I and the Turks which had been broken upon the instigation of the papacy with disastrous consequences for Wladislav and Western Christendom, Luther says: "If there were no other evil wiles

with Luther, who believed that the God of history must and will punish those who trespass against his eternal moral law.[43]

When the Conciliar Movement failed and when the appeals for a free general council found deaf ears in Rome, the last chance to reunite Western Christendom was lost. The responsibility for this catastrophe does not lie with the Protestant reformers but with the men in Rome whose insatiable pride preferred the disruption of Christianity to a genuine reformation which might have curtailed their power.

. . . .

to prove the pope the true Anti-Christ, yet this one thing were enough to prove it. Hearest thou this, O pope, not most holy, but most sinful? . . . God has commanded to keep oath and faith even with an enemy, and thou undertakest to loose this His commandment and ordainest in thine heretical, Anti-christian decretals that thou hast His power. . . . In olden times the children of Israel had to keep the oath which they had unwittingly been deceived into giving to their enemies, the Gibeonites, and King Zedekiah was miserably lost, with all his people because he broke his oath to the king of Babylon. Even among us, a hundred years ago, that fine king of Hungary and Poland, Wladislav, was slain by the Turk, with so many noble people, because he allowed himself to be deceived by the papal legate and cardinal, and broke the good and advantageous treaty which he had sworn with the Turk. The pious Emperor Sigismund had no good fortune after the Council of Constance, when he allowed the knaves to break the safe-conduct which had been given to John Hus and Jerome, and all the trouble between us and the Bohemians was the consequence. Even in our own times, God help us! how much Christian blood has been shed over the oath and alliance which Pope Julius made between the Emperor Maximilian and King Louis of France, and afterwards broke? How could I tell all the troubles which the popes have stirred up by the devilish presumption with which they annul oaths and vows which have been made between great princes, making a jest of these things, and taking money for it. I have hopes that the judgment day is at the door; nothing can possibly be worse than the Roman See." Phila. Ed., II, 138 ff.

IV. THE METHODOLOGICAL PRINCIPLE

In the previous chapter it has been shown that the allegation that Luther caused or even encouraged capitalism and nationalism cannot be substantiated. If he made any contribution in the realm of social ethics, this contribution must be found in another direction. Here it is of the greatest importance to discover the method which Luther used in discussing social-ethical problems and the ethical standards as they apply to society.

This, of course, raises the question of whether Luther had any method at all.[1] There are those who speak with enthusiasm of Luther's "religious genius" but deny that any unifying method underlies his writings.[2] But even those authors who grant that Luther made a theological contribution will often agree with Tawney that "Luther's utterances

. . . .

[1] To the following see Philip S. Watson, *Let God be God,* Philadelphia, 1948, and Joseph Sittler, Jr., *The Doctrine of the Word,* Philadelphia, 1948.

[2] See Sidney Cave, *The Doctrine of the Person of Christ,* London, 1925, p. 148.

[3] Tawney, p. 79. See also Gerhard Ritter, *Encyclopaedia of the Social Sciences,* Macmillan, 1942, IX, 631. "Not the conquest and mastery of the world by Christianity, not the transformation of its culture and society by the Christian idea, not the organization of a powerful World-Church, is the essential intention of this monastic ascetic, but the reconciliation of the individual soul with its God. From this arises a religious ethics of the individual which it is very difficult to broaden into a social ethics. . . . His (Luther's) works reveal no mention of ideas of social reform." See also George E. Catlin, *The Story of the Political Philosophers,* New York, 1939, p. 213: "Luther, himself a spiritual Henry VIII, contributes no coherent political theory."

[4] Heinrich Boehmer, *Luther and the Reformation in the Light of Modern Research,* London, 1930, p. 248, asserts that Luther

on social morality are the occasional explosions of a capricious volcano . . . and it is idle to scan them for a coherent and consistent doctrine."[3]

In order to understand this view of the irrational character of Luther's thought, which is held by many friends and foes of the reformer,[4] it is necessary to keep in mind that Luther's thought has been generally interpreted by German scholars.[5] Even the non-German authors who deal with Luther's theology or ethics are largely dependent upon the secondary material supplied by such men as Troeltsch and Denifle. This reliance on German secondary sources has utterly confused the issue, since German scholars by their training and the exigencies of their occupation (if they are university professors) are in no position to interpret Luther's thought objectively. The German university professor is a system builder, and he will invariably attempt to integrate history into his system. For him only a systematic method in

. . . .

"had never been trained to pay attention to the connection between religious and theological concepts, to organize and bring them into relation with one another, or even merely to collate them." He continues, "Consequently, we are, even with the best of intentions, unable to discover a strict consistency in his system, indeed we can in no way forcibly bind his views together into a logical structure." (p. 250) See also the similar views expressed by the Swedish scholars, Runestam, Bohlin, and Aulen (Edgar M. Carlson, *The Reinterpretation of Luther*, Philadelphia, 1948, p. 54). Maritain, *Three Reformers*, pp. 28-29, takes great pains to show the "anti-intellectualism" of Luther, confusing always the attacks of Luther against the "saving reason" of the scholastics with an attack against reason as such. Maritain says, "From him (Luther) Carlstadt, as early as 1518 borrowed that fine thought, that 'logic is nowhere necessary in theology because Christ does not need human inventions!'" Maritain neglects to tell the source of his information that Carlstadt borrowed this view from Luther.

[5] During the last thirty years Scandinavian authors have begun to take the leadership in Luther research. However, most of

which all dialectic antitheses are ultimately resolved in a more comprehensive synthesis deserves the name of method. These systems must be original, preferably distinguished by their own vocabulary, and must use the thoughts of other men as mere building blocks in the erection of the new system.[6] If the thought of a theologian of the past does not fit into the framework of the system, the task of the scholar becomes very similar to that of a stonecutter who toils on a piece of marble until he has shaped it into the form that will make it fit properly into the structure that is to be erected. In the process the shape of the raw marble block may have been completely changed and most of the marble may be among the waste.

For this type of "systematic" scholarship which has been much admired and imitated all over the world, Luther

. . . .

their writings have not been available in English and have only slowly made an impact outside the Scandinavian countries. For an American interpretation of the Scandinavian Luther research see Edgar Carlson. In England, Philip S. Watson, op.cit., shows the wholesome influence of the new trend.

[6] For a fascinating summary of this tendency by one of the great contemporary system-builders see Karl Barth, *Die protestantische Theologie im 19. Jahrhundert*, Zürich, 1947, p. 5 ff. Barth lists as examples among others Ernst Troeltsch, W. Herrmann, W. Elert, Emil Brunner, and the Jesuit, E. Przywara.

[7] This may be the reason for the fact that each generation of Germans has been able to describe Luther in terms that made the reformer the champion of their own ideas and ideals. Lutheran orthodoxy saw in Luther the church-father and the inexhaustible source of prooftexts. The pietistic movement found him a courageous fighter against priestcraft. The men of the Enlightenment considered Luther an honest defender of the freedom of conscience. Later, when German nationalism was born out of the experience of the Napoleonic wars, Luther was understood to be the first great national hero. The scientific nineteenth century admired his contribution to a more scientific exegesis of the Bible. The dialectic theology turned to Luther as

proved most unwieldy material.[7] Luther's thought, which is "existential," starting not with a system but with life, proved singularly intractable to this scholastic method.[8] Luther, whose theological and ethical aim was to describe and interpret the relationship of man to God and God's creation, cared little whether the result was systematic or not, as long as he felt that it described the actual human situation. He felt a deep disgust for those "Sophists," as he called the scholastic philosophers, for whom thought preceded life and who constructed wonderfully balanced systems whose only drawback was that they were not true.[9] It was against these comfortable scholastic metaphysicians that Luther insisted on phrasing thoughts in a seemingly self-contradictory manner. He said: "A Christian man is a perfectly free lord of all, subject to none," and continued

. . . .

a dialectic thinker. National Socialism re-edited and published his more acrimonious writings against the Jews, calling Luther the man who had first realized the terrible danger that threatened the world from the Jews. Since the war, Luther has become exhibit number one for those of the Vansittart-Morgenthau mentality, proving the basic corruption of the German race. See Boehmer, op. cit., pp. 1-40; H. Stephan, *Luther in den Wandlungen seiner Kirche,* Giessen, 1907.

[8] For a study of the "existential" character of Luther's thought see Lennart Pinomaa, *Der existentielle Character der Theologie Luthers,* Helsinki, 1940.

[9] W.A.T., 4, 380, (4567): "No Sophist was able to interpret correctly the words, 'the just shall live by faith'; even the fathers failed to understand it, with the exception of Augustine. So much blindness was even among the dear fathers. Therefore we should first of all read Holy Scripture, then also the fathers—but with moderation, for they do not always judge rightly concerning the affairs of God." See also W.A., 7, 449, 32 (Cause and Reasons, 1521): "It is not right to play with words when dealing with serious and important matters. This easily deceives simple minds and such teachers are called Sophists." See also his specific references to Thomas Aquinas and Peter Lombard.

immediately, "A Christian man is a perfectly dutiful servant of all, subject to all."[10] This was not an attempt at sparkling dialectics, where seeming contradictions are presented only to resolve them in some great all-embracing synthesis, but merely an effort to describe man's actual relationships in life.

Luther said that the Christian man is a sinner and righteous at the same time.[11] He did not make this statement because of its systematic utility but rather because it described for him the actual relationship of man to God. Here also belongs his simultaneous insistence upon the immanence and transcendence of God, which he expressed most effectively in one of his Christmas hymns: "He who

. . . .

About the former, Luther said: "He has written much that is heretical and is responsible for the rule of Aristotle, who is the destroyer of all sound doctrine." (W.A., 8, 127, 19, Rationis Latomianae Confutatio, 1521) And in another place he said: "In all of the works of Thomas Aquinas there isn't one word that would give one confidence in Christ." (W.A.T., 2, 193, 1721) His judgments concerning Peter Lombard were more sympathetic. He said: "He was a great man; had he only applied himself to the Bible he would have been doubtlessly the greatest." (W.A.T., 1, 85, 17) Later he said: "He (Peter Lombard) read through all authors, Hilary, Augustine, Ambrose, Gregory, and Jerome, and in addition all the reports of councils and all decretals. Had he applied the same amount of industry to the Bible, things would have worked out. Well, it was not supposed to be." (W.A.T., 2, 517, 13, 2544 b) Luther is particularly opposed to Duns Scotus and his claims that man can love God out of his own natural power above everything. He says: "It is certainly true that those arguments are the weakest which reason from man to God, as Scotus is wont to do. Man, he says, can love God above everything because he loves himself above everything. It follows that he can love God much more since the greater good is also much more lovable. From this Scotus infers that man can fulfill this highest command out of his own natural power." (W.A., 40, I, 459, 31, Commentary on Galatians, 1535) Here Luther shows clearly that his objection is not to the use of reason but to the prostitution of reason by the scholastic theolo-

48

could not be contained by the Universe is now held in the arms of Mary, and He has become a small infant although He alone upholds everything that is."[12] Similarly, Luther's seemingly irrational insistence upon the real presence of the body and blood of Christ in the sacrament of the Lord's Supper in his controversy with Zwingli was not an expression of "biblicism," but the result of his belief that Zwingli's spiritualization of this sacrament detracted as much from the reality of God's self-communication as the sacramental magic of the Roman mass.[13]

The examples could be multiplied with his attitude towards the law, the devil, sin, free will, etc., and it will show

. . . .

gians. Duns Scotus' claim that man who loves the smaller good, must be able to love the greater good even more is for Luther the perfect illustration of the fruitlessness of the scholastic method. A logical deduction takes the place of life, and the result is a complete misunderstanding of the human situation. This is the type of system that Luther cannot tolerate.

[10] Phila. Ed., II, 312 (A Treatise on Christian Liberty, 1520).

[11] W.A., 40, I, 368 (Comm. Gal.): "Thus a Christian is at the same time righteous and sinner, saint and profane, enemy and son of God. These antitheses the Sophists will not admit because they do not understand the meaning of justification." See also W.A., 40, I, 370, 19 (Comm. Gal.): "Christian righteousness is, as we have said, that righteousness which God counts as righteousness because of the faith in Christ or for Christ's sake. When the Sophists hear this wonderful description which is unknown to reason, they deride it because they imagine that righteousness is a quality which has first to be infused and then to be distributed to all the members. They cannot free themselves from the ideas of reason which pretend that correct insights and a correct will are the same as righteousness."

[12] W.A., 35, 434, 12 ff. (Luther's Hymns).

[13] Cf. P. W. Genrich, *Die Christologie Luthers im Abendmahlsstreit*, Göttingen, 1929. See also George W. Forell, "The Lord's Supper and Christology," *Lutheran Church Quarterly*, XVIII, 1945, pp. 91 ff.

itself in the discussion of his social ethics as well. Luther knew that if man desires to describe the revelation of God, he will often find the paradox the only adequate means of expression. And he did not hesitate to use this means because of the objections from those theologians that hoped to be able to squeeze the truth of God into the strait jacket of the logical system of Aristotle.[14] Luther's method of describing man's relationship to God in terms of actual life, with all the complexities which that involves, forced those scholars who insist on using only that part of a man's thought which fits into their system, discarding the rest as inconsequential, to suppress a great deal of Luther. At the same time, there was hardly a man who could not use some of Luther's thought to fortify his own position. The resulting confusion in regard to the interpretation of Luther's theology was not so much in Luther as in the men who explained him to the world.

One flagrant example of the results of the German quest for original systems as it affects the interpretation of Luther's social ethics may help to illustrate this point. Ernst Troeltsch is widely acclaimed as the most authoritative writer on the

. . . .

[14] Cf. D. M. Baillie, *God Was in Christ,* New York, 1948, pp. 108-09: "The reason why the element of paradox comes into all religious thought and statement is because God cannot be comprehended in any human words or in any of the categories of our finite thought. . . . The attempt to put our experiences of God into theological statements is something like the attempt to draw a map of the world on a flat surface, the page of an atlas. It is impossible to do this without a certain degree of falsification, because the surface of the earth is a spherical surface whose pattern cannot be reproduced accurately upon a plane. . . . Therefore an atlas meets the problem by giving us two different maps of the world which can be compared with each other. The one is contained in two circles representing two hemispheres. The other is contained in an oblong. Each is a map of the whole world, and they contradict each other to some extent at every point. Yet they are both needed and taken

50

history of Christian social teachings. However, it is easily shown that Troeltsch, the German university professor, approached the subject with a preconceived notion around which history was to be arranged. He holds the view that the history of Christendom shows the contrast between two types of Christianity, the Church type and the sect type.[15] According to Troeltsch's system, Luther belongs to the Church type and must therefore show the characteristics which Troeltsch has established as typical for the Church. Among these characteristics is the important tendency to water down the absolute ethical demands of the Sermon on the Mount because of their impractical nature. According to Troeltsch, the Church-Christian will interpret the Sermon on the Mount in terms of the Decalogue, thus making it universally useful, while the Sect-Christian will insist on the absolute demands of the Sermon on the Mount. Since Luther is a "Church founder" he must have reduced the demands of the Sermon on the Mount in terms of the Decalogue.[16] Troeltsch's assertion is a logical deduction from the presuppositions of his system.[17] Yet every child that ever memorized Luther's Small Catechism could have told him that the

. . . .

together they correct each other. . . . So it is with the paradoxes of faith. They are inevitable, not because the divine reality is self-contradictory, but because when we objectify it all our judgments are in some measure falsified, and the higher truth which reconciles them cannot be fully expressed in words. . . ."

[15] Troeltsch, *Social Teachings,* I, 331 ff.

[16] Troeltsch, II, 508.

[17] Cf. Karl Holl. *Gesammelte Aufsätze,* I, 248. After quoting Troeltsch, Holl says: "This is one of the passages where it becomes most obvious to me that Troeltsch arrives at his judgments not on the basis of the sources but under the compulsion of previously established concepts. Since this is the way in which things ought to work in a 'church' it must have worked in this manner in the case of Luther. He is a 'church-founder' and as such he must reduce the standards of morality. Yet any explana-

exact opposite is the case and that in Luther's explanation of the Ten Commandments, these commandments are consistently interpreted in terms of the Sermon on the Mount.[18]

If as competent and learned a scholar as Ernst Troeltsch fell victim to this professorial tendency, it cannot cause any surprise that there are actually as many Luthers as there are German professors discussing Luther, and that each one of them, even his staunchest defender, suppresses that part of Luther's thinking which conflicts with his respective system. Thus Luther, who even during his lifetime had felt the attacks of the systematizers,[19] was after his death buried among the writings of men whom he himself had called sarcastically *Sau-theologen,* the men with the system.[20]

. . . .

tion of the Ten Commandments found within the Lutheran tradition—I am satisfied to take only the Small Catechism—shows that the Sermon on the Mount is here not reinterpreted in terms of the Decalogue but on the contrary the Decalogue is reinterpreted in terms of the Sermon on the Mount. I would further like to point out that some of the most daring remarks of Luther concerning the Decalogue were made after 1532. . . . This is indeed a different Luther than the one created according to the wishes of Troeltsch. I won't even go into the 'Jewish moral wisdom' which Luther is supposed to have utilized. This Troeltsch has freely invented." However, it must be admitted that Holl has also done his share of systematic reinterpretation of Luther in terms of his own philosophical presuppositions. Cf. Franz Lau, *Aüsserliche Ordnung und Weltlich Ding in Luthers Theologie,* Göttingen, 1933.

[18] See Martin Luther, *The Small Catechism* in H. E. Jacobs, *The Book of Concord,* Philadelphia, 1908, p. 365: "The Fifth Commandment. Thou shalt not kill. What is meant by this Commandment? Answer. We should so fear and love God as not to do our neighbor any bodily harm or injury, but rather assist and comfort him in danger and want. . . . The Eighth Commandment. Thou shalt not bear false witness against thy neighbor. What is meant by this commandment? Answer. We should so fear and love God as not deceitfully to belie, betray,

For an understanding of Luther's thought it was of tragic importance that the minds of the Germans to whom Luther spoke first and to whom he was most immediately accessible were soon ruled by people who were quite out of sympathy with Luther's concern with life, and who much preferred a systematic discussion of thought. The theologian, who was vitally concerned with God's deeds for man, fell among the metaphysicians, who cared only about man's thoughts about God.

This is the reason for the alleged "irrationalism" of Luther's thought. It is quite true that Luther made many disrespectful statements about human reason.[21] They have been frequently quoted. But Luther made as many, if not

. . . .

slander, nor raise injurious reports against our neighbor, but apologize for him, speak well of him, and put the most charitable construction on all his actions."

[19] W.A., 50, 547, 17 ff. (Of Councils and Churches, 1539). Cf. Phila. Ed., V, 174 ff: "I take up the saying of St. Hilary's, De trinitate, Ex causis dicendis summenda est intelligentia dictorum, i.e., 'He who will understand what is said must see why or for what reasons it is said.' Sic ex causis agendi cognoscuntur acta. The natural reason teaches the same thing. . . . Thus there are many sayings in the Scriptures which, taken literally, are contradictory, but if the causes are shown, everything is right. . . . What indeed is the whole life of man, except mere antilogiae, or 'contradictions,' until one hears the causes. My antilogists, therefore, are great, fine, pious sows and asses. They collect my antilogies and let the causes alone. . . ."

[20] W.A., 56, 274, 11 ff. (Comm. Romans, 1515).

[21] W.A., 18, 164 (Against the "Heavenly" Prophets): "Furthermore, he (Carlstadt) teaches us what 'Frau Hulde,' our natural reason, has to say to these things. As if we did not know that reason is the whore of the devil and can do nothing but desecrate and detract from all God says and does." See also W.A., 51, 126, 27 (Sermon for the Second Sunday after Epiphany, January 17, 1546): "Usury, drunkenness, adultery, murder, homicide, etc. —such actions are noticed and even the world comprehends that

more, complimentary statements about human reason which are hardly ever mentioned.[22] Here again he was describing reason in two different relationships. When reason was used as a means to attain God, as in scholastic philosophy, he would call it the "whore of the devil." When reason was used as a tool in the service of God,[23] he would recommend its careful and conscientious use as a glorious divine gift.

Here Luther's methodological principle becomes clear. Actions, faculties, beings, and standards are good or evil not

. . . .

they are sins. But the devil's bride, reason, the beautiful harlot, comes in and acts smart. Whatever she says she considers said by the Holy Spirit. Who can help here? Neither lawyer, doctor, king, nor emperor. This devil's whore is the worst of all. The other crass sins are noticed but reason is judged by no one."

[22] W.A., 48, 76 (Inscriptions): "Reason is also a light and a beautiful light. But the road that leads from sin and death to righteousness and life reason cannot find and it remains in darkness. Just as our lanterns and candles do not lighten heaven and earth but the dark corners in homes, but the sun gives his light to heaven and earth and shines everywhere, so God's Word is the true sun, which gives us the eternal day so that we may live and rejoice." See also W.A., 39, I, 175, 9 ff. (Disputation Concerning Man, 1536): "It is indeed true that reason is the principal and most important possession of all. It is above all things of this life the best and something divine. Reason is the inventor and ruler of all arts, of medicine, law, and all wisdom, might, virtue, and honor which men can possess in this life. Indeed, reason must be called the essential difference by which man is distinguished from the animals and other things. Holy Scripture makes reason a ruler over the earth, its birds and fishes and cattle, saying "rule." This means reason is a kind of sun and divinity given for the administration of the things of this life. And this majesty God has not taken from reason after Adam's fall, but rather confirmed it."

[23] W.A., 10, 207, 5 ff. (Kirchenpostille, 1522): "For there is not a man found in whom there is not the natural light of reason, from which cause alone he is called man and is worthy

in a static sense, so that if their value is once described it will hold true forever, but in a dynamic sense, i.e., according to their function of helping or hindering the all-important relationship between God and man. Just as reason is "good" if used in order to rule justly and "bad" if it is a tool of man to conquer God,[24] so "good works" are "good" if they are the fruit of the Spirit and "evil" if they are used as means to buy salvation.[25]

This dynamic character of Luther's evaluation is also

. . . .

to be a man."

[24] W.A., 42, 107, 27 ff. (Comm. Genesis, 1535): "Against this the Sophists quote the statement of Aristotle that reason leads us always to do the best. And they attempt to substantiate this assertion with statements of Holy Scripture. Especially do they quote the claim of the philosophers that right reason is the cause of all virtues. I do not deny this if it is understood to apply to those matters which are subject to reason, as, for example, the raising of cattle, the building of houses, the planting of fields; however, it is not true as far as the higher things of life are concerned. How is it possible to call this reason righteous which hates God? How can we call that will good which resists the will of God and refuses to obey Him? Therefore when they say, 'Reason leads us always to do the best,' you may answer, 'Yes indeed; in the matters belonging to civil righteousness about which reason can judge, it does speak and judge and guide us to honor and to those things which are useful from a physical and worldly point of view.'" See also ibid., 291, 30: "Without the Holy Spirit reason is simply without all knowledge of God. And to be without knowledge of God means to be godless, to live in darkness and to judge those things to be the best which are in fact the worst. I am talking here about 'the good' theologically and the distinction must be made between 'society in general' (politia) and 'theology.' For God approves even the political rule of the godless and decorates and rewards their virtues. But this applies only as far as this life goes, and as far as reason in general is concerned. It does not extend to the life to come."

[25] W.A., 25, 324, 1 (Lectures on Isaiah, 1527-1529): "They err who claim that Christ is a lawgiver who gives moral counsel

shown in his attitude towards the devil, who is the rebellious force of evil, tempting and murdering even the Son of

. . . .

and like Socrates presents perfect examples of virtue. For, although He does also form our outward actions, He first of all renews the inner man. Afterwards He rules also the body, hands, and feet. For faith is followed by works as the body is followed by its shadow." W.A., 44, 135, 2 (Lectures on Genesis): "I do not pray or meditate in the Law of the Lord all the time. I do not fight constantly against sin, death, and devil; on the contrary, I get dressed, I sleep, I play with the children, I eat and drink, etc. Yet all these works if done in faith are considered by God 'well done' and approved according to His divine judgment." W.A., 33, 168 (Sermon on John 6:48): "We should not simply think, 'All I have to do is to believe and everything is taken care of, I do not have to do any good works.' No, we must not separate the two. You must do good works and help your neighbor so that faith may shine outwardly in life as it shines inwardly in the heart." On the other hand, see also W.A., 40, II, 11, 18 (Comm. Gal. 1535): "This makes it sufficiently clear that in all the world nothing is more dangerous than these doctrines concerning human traditions and works. They undo and pervert the true faith of the Gospel and the true worship of God. . . . Therefore, he who initiates and cultivates a doctrine of works oppresses the Gospel and makes the death and victory of Christ useless; he obscures His sacraments and destroys their use. Such a person denies, blasphemes, and opposes God and all His promises and benefits." W.A., 5, 31, 19 (Comm. Psalms, 1519): "But you may say, 'How can the works of the Jews, heretics, and the proud be evil? They fast, pray, do good works and other things of which nobody would dare say that they are evil.' I have said that faith is necessary. Therefore these works make things worse, since they confirm their godlessness and help them stand fast and persevere in the path of sin. Their works are sins since they proceed from a godless heart."

[26] The independent power of the devil to do evil is often noted by Luther. W.A., 34, II, 232, 28 (Sermon of September 28, 1531): "For this reason Christ calls the devil the 'prince of this world,' his power is greater than that of the Turkish emperors,

God,[26] and yet is God's devil and thus ultimately subject to the power of the Divine will.[27]

. . . .

his intelligence is above all human intelligence, his malice is beyond all human malice." Ibid., 235, 22: "Therefore we must not follow the example of the pagans who have made good fortune into a goddess and attribute all events to her. On the contrary, we Christians ought to know that we are in the world and the kingdom of the devil, where there are many thousand devils. And whatever evil befalls us we ought to recognize as the result of the devil's activity." W.A., 52, 716, 14 (Hauspostille, St. Michael's Day, 1544): "For you have heard it often that the devil surrounds men everywhere. He is at the courts of princes, in homes, on fields, on every street, on water, in woods, in fire. In short: Everything is full of devils who do nothing else than try every instant to break people's necks. And it is certainly true that if God would not defend us against this evil enemy without ceasing, the devil would not leave one kernel of grain, neither fish nor meat, neither water, beer, nor wine without poisoning it." See also W.A.T., 3, 596 (3763): "The devil is most powerful in this world. Great is his power, therefore he is called a god and the prince of this world." W.A.T., 1, 151 (360): "This devil is the author of death and of all pestilence and disease." This power of the devil extends even over God's saints. Luther says: "The power of the devil is revealed in the fall of the saints. How powerful the devil, the prince of this world, is does not become clear in the downfall of worldly people and those who are wise in the ways of the world . . . but rather in the saints, who had received the Holy Spirit. As, e.g., Adam, David, Peter, etc., who committed great and crude sins and fell." W.A.T., 1, 485 (958). This power of the devil reaches its limit in his attempt to extend it over Christ, the incarnate Son of God. Only here does he overreach himself. Luther says: "I beheld once a wolf tearing sheep. When the wolf comes into a sheepfold, he eats not any until he has killed all, and then he begins to eat, thinking to devour all. Even so it is also with the devil; I have now, thinks he, taken hold on Christ, and in time will also snap his disciples. But the devil's folly is that he sees not he has to do with the Son of God; he knows not that in the end it will be his bane. It will come to pass, that the devil must

57

This functional evaluation perhaps becomes clearest in Luther's view of the law. The law is good if used to achieve

. . . .

be afraid of a child in the cradle for when he but hears the name Jesus, uttered in true faith, then he cannot stay. The devil would rather run through the fire, than stay where Christ is; therefore it is justly said: 'The seed of the woman shall crush the serpent's head.' I believe indeed, He has so crushed his head, that he can neither abide to see nor hear Christ Jesus. I often delight myself with that similitude in Job, of an angle-hook that fishermen cast into the water, putting on the hook a little worm; then comes the fish and snatches at the worm, and gets therewith the hook in his jaws, and the fisher pulls him out of the water. Even so has our Lord God dealt with the devil; God has cast into the world his only Son, as the angle, and upon the hook has put Christ's humanity, as the worm; then comes the devil and snaps at the (man) Christ, and devours him, and therewith he bites the iron hook, that is, the godhead of Christ, which chokes him, and all his power thereby is thrown to the ground. This is called sapientia divina, divine wisdom." (*Table-Talk*, tr. William Hazlitt, London, 1902, CXCVII.

[27] W.A., 16, 10, 12 (Sermon on Exodus, October 2, 1524): "Thus God acts against the world and the devil's wrath and commotion. Their tyranny, their destruction and anger do not only fail to hurt the Gospel but on the contrary they help to advance and spread it, and the devil and the world break their heads smashing into the Gospel." W.A., 18, 710, 31 (On the Bondage of the Will, 1525): "Nobody should think that God, when it is said of Him that He 'hardens' and 'works evil in us' (for to harden is to work evil), acts in such a manner as if He created a new evil in us. He is not like a malicious tavern-keeper who is himself evil and pours or mixes poison into a vessel which is not evil, so that the vessel does nothing but receive and suffer the malice of the poisoner. This is how they seem to imagine that man, who is in himself good or at least not evil, suffers an evil deed from God when they hear that we say that God works in us both the good and the evil. We are supposed to believe that man is subjected to God by necessity and is entirely passive. They give not enough thought to the

58

the civil justice which is necessary for the maintenance of life among men. Luther has much to say about this "political

. . . .

fact that God works restlessly in all His creatures and that none is ever idle. Anybody who wants to understand what it means that God works in us (i.e., through us) must reason as follows: What happens does not happen as the result of God's fault but as a result of our own. Since we are by nature evil, God by nature good, He moves through His almighty power. And He who Himself is good will do evil through an evil tool. Nevertheless, according to His wisdom, He uses even the evil to His glory and for our salvation. Likewise, He finds the will of the devil evil, but He did not create it thus. But when God left him and the devil sinned, he became evil. Now God drives the devil through His power and moves him to his actions. Yet this will of the devil does not cease to be evil because of God's moving power." W.A.T., 1, 347, 33 (722): "When godlessness and all kinds of sins take over in the world, the devil must be God's hangman." *Table-Talk*, Hazlitt, DCXVI: "God gives to the devil and to witches power over human creatures in two ways: first, over the ungodly, when He will punish them by reason of their sins; secondly, over the just and godly, when He intends to try whether they will be constant in the faith, and remain in His obedience. Without God's will and our own consent, the devil cannot hurt us; for God says: 'Whoso touches you, toucheth the apple of mine eye.' And Christ: 'There cannot fall a hair from our head, without your heavenly Father's notice.'" W.A., 40, II, 519 (Exposition of the 90th Psalm, 1534-35): "God, indeed, uses the devil to afflict us and kill us, but the devil could not do that if God did not wish to punish sin in this manner." See also the influence of this thinking upon German literature and Goethe. In *Faust,* Basel, 1944, I, 174, Mephistopheles says of himself that he is "Ein Teil von jener Kraft, die stets das Boese will und stets das Gute schafft." See the following quotations from Luther's writings: W.A., 16, 9, 14 (Sermon on Exodus, October 2, 1524): "And this is what the dear Gospel does: wherever it is revealed, all the plans of the tyrants must collapse. Though they plot how to hinder the advance of the Gospel, they must learn that no wisdom, power, or force helps against the Word of God. It advances and overthrows everything that bars use" of the law,[28] especially against the "Antinomians" who wanted to do away with the law altogether. But while the law in this civil function is useful and good, its theological function is purely negative. The law not only reveals man's

. . . .

its way. Just as water may be kept in a lake by damming up the outlet, yet the water will collect and the lake will rise until it finally finds a hole in the dam where it will break through, or the lake overflows and overruns the dam, for the water will not be stopped and must take its way. In like manner, the devil and the world oppose the dear Gospel, try to stop it by hindering preachers and listeners, and use all kinds of tyranny and persecution. All this is to no avail. The divine Word takes its course even if devil and world should for this reason lose their mind." That Luther's view must finally be understood from his conviction of God's ultimate will to save is shown wherever Luther tries to reconcile God's omnipotence and His love. Cf. W.A., 40, III, 584, 31 (Exp. 90th Psalm): "Isaiah makes here a distinction and says that some works are God's works, but His foreign works, others are His proper works. His proper works are the works of mercy, where He forgives sins, declares righteous, and saves those who believe in Christ. His foreign works are those where He judges, condemns, and punishes the unrepentant and unbelieving. These latter God has to take upon Himself and call His works because of our pride, so that we might be humbled, recognize Him as our Lord, and obey His will."

[28] W.A., 17, I, 122 (Sermon on I Timothy 1:8-11, March 28, 1525): "As I see it, St. Paul answers here as follows: I confess that the law is good, but it isn't so good that many people do not misuse it or use it badly. It is good if it is used correctly, it is not good but harmful when it is not used correctly." W.A., 40, I, 620, 31 (Comm. Gal., 1535): "We know that the law is good if used correctly (I Tim. 1:8). This means that the law exists for the benefit of society (politice) to keep evil people in line, and theologically speaking (theologice) to point up sin. But whoever uses the law to attain righteousness before God does not know what he is saying and makes the good law a source of danger and damnation for himself." W.A., 40, I, 558, 24 (Comm. Gal.): "Except in relation to justification we must think reverently about the law, give it highest honors and call it

60

sin but if it is used by man to establish the relationship with God, it actually drives him deeper into sin.[29] Far from being the static good of all legalistic religion, the law can become for Luther a severe temptation and a soul-destroying

. . . .

'just,' 'good,' 'spiritual,' 'divine,' etc. Outside of the conscience we must make it into a god; in relation to conscience, however, it is truly a devil." W.A., 40, II, 177, 36 (Comm. Gal.): "Are the laws therefore evil? No, on the contrary they are good and useful, but in their proper order and place. This means they are adequate in physical and civil matters where nothing can be administered without laws." Cf. also Axel Gyllenkrok, *Rechtfertigung und Heiligung in der frühen evangelischen Theologie Luthers*, Uppsala, 1952. He points out that this functional method of Luther means that "law" and "Gospel" are essentially the same but looked at from different points of view. Gyllenkrok quotes statements from Luther's early works which indicate that the law spiritually understood is the same as the Gospel. (pp. 31 ff.) See also W.A., 3, 96, 26 ff. (Comm. Psalms, 1513-16).

[29] W.A., 5, 216, 32 ff. (Comm. Psalms, 1519-21): "For the law worketh wrath, as St. Paul says (Rom. 4:15), because it revealeth sin, by which the conscience is confounded; it is distressed and put in perturbation by wrath and death, which the soul sees that it deserves by the law revealing them. This excess, when men fall into it, suddenly and terribly vexes and confounds and disturbs the proud, bringing them to nothing and forcing them to lay aside all supercilious conceit of their own righteousness and to seek the mercy of God." (Tr. Lenker) W.A., 5, 323, 3 ff. (Comm. Psalms, 1519-21): "Through the law comes the knowledge of sin." (Rom. 3:20) Again: "The law worketh wrath." (Rom. 4:15) And I Corinthians 15:56: "The strength of sin is the law. For there is no other reason for the endless pride of the godless than that they are as yet unable to understand the law and its power. They do not know that it is 'spiritual' and kills through its letter all men." W.A., 2, 499, 34 ff. (Comm. Gal. 1519): "The law of the letter is that law which is written with letters, expressed in words, considered in thoughts. . . . This is the law of works, the old law, the law of Moses, the law of the flesh, of sin, of wrath, of death; it condemns every-

power destined to drive man to despair and ever further away from God.[30]

Luther refused to recognize any permanent and unalterable ethical standards if these existed in a religious vacuum. The ethical standards of the pagan philosophers he considered "lies" and "godless fables."[31] All ethical standards are meaningful only in life. They are good if they serve to reveal God; they are evil if they hide God from men. Actions, faculties, beings, and standards are good or evil according to the function which they fulfill in helping or hindering the establishment of the saving relationship between God and man. Thus it is Luther's concern to evaluate everything in relation to God and His revelation in Jesus Christ. And for Luther the center of this revelation of God in Christ is the Gospel of the forgiveness of sins. Without this forgiveness of sins, a saving relationship between God and man would be impossible.

Any ethical assertion implies the existence of certain standards of right and wrong upon which the assertion is

. . . .

thing and makes everybody guilty, it increases lust and kills." W.A., 5, 500, 16 (Comm. Psalms, 1519-21): "It is the work of the law to terrify, to upset the conscience, and to demolish all trust." See also W.A., 5, 508, 15 ff; W.A., 18, 684, 29; W.A., 39, I, 385, 17 ff.

[30] W.A., 40, I, 554 (Comm. Gal., 1535): "Furthermore, even if used for the best purpose the law can do nothing but accuse, terrify, condemn, and kill. Where there is fear and awareness of sin, death, and the wrath of God, there is certainly no righteousness, nothing heavenly, nothing divine, but only things of this world. But this world is nothing else but a sewer of sin, death, the wrath of God, hell, and of all evil. This is felt by the fearful and depressed but is not felt by those who consider themselves secure and by scorners. For this reason the law, even in its best use, can only lead to the recognition of sin and to the fear of death. But sin, death, and other evils are indeed worldly things. Thus it is obvious that the law does not give life, salvation, or anything heavenly or divine, but only earthly things." See also

based, and any assertion of Christian ethics implies that it is God who has given these standards. Christian ethics is based upon the claim that a saving relationship between God and man is possible. Such a claim can only be made on the basis of the Gospel of the forgiveness of sins.[32]

As far as Luther is concerned, all ethics is based upon God's forgiveness of sin. This is true of individual ethics as well as social ethics. It is therefore meaningless to say that Luther considered the Sermon on the Mount the Christian standard for individual ethics while he suggested the Decalogue or some other form of natural law as the standard for social ethics.[33] Neither the Sermon on the Mount nor the Decalogue is the point of reference for Luther's ethics, but always the relationship which God establishes with man through the forgiveness of sins in love. The Decalogue or the Sermon on the Mount, if interpreted apart from this point of reference, may become for Luther not the will of God but the will of the devil. Any use of ethical standards divorced from their source perverts these standards

. . . .

W.A., 40, I, 487, 15 ff; W.A., 10, I, 223, 33 ff.

31] W.A., 5, 137 (Comm. Psalms, 1519-21): "Hence it comes to pass that they most miserably crucify and murder the people by their lies and godless fables which they take from the morals of the philosophers, the laws of men, and their own precepts and traditions. . . ."

32] W.A., 40, III, 351, 33 (Comm. Psalms, 1532-33): "In these two verses (concerning the forgiveness of sins) David submits a summary of the entire Christian doctrine and shows the sun which illuminates the church. If this doctrine stands, the Church will stand; if it falls, then the Church must also fall." W.A., 40, II, 359 (Comm. Psalms, 1532-33): "This conclusion I call to your attention: Where there is no forgiveness there is no God; where there is no God there is no forgiveness. And where there is no forgiveness there is no fear or worship of God, but only idolatry and work-righteousness."

33] Cf. Troeltsch, II, 508.

from good into evil.[34]

This central importance of the relationship of God to man as established by the Gospel of the forgiveness of sins is the key to Luther's method. But this "dynamic" method of Luther,[35] though in sharp contrast to the dialectical method of the scholastics, Catholic and Protestant, is a method nevertheless. As Einar Billing has said, "Whoever knows Luther even but partially, knows that his various thoughts do not lie alongside each other, like pearls on a string, held together only by common authority or perchance by a line of logical argument, but that they all, as tightly as the petals of a rosebud, adhere to a common center, and radiate out like the rays of the sun from one glowing core, namely the gospel of the forgiveness of sins. Anyone wishing to study Luther would indeed be in no peril of going astray were he to follow this rule: never believe that you have a correct understanding of a thought of Luther before you have succeeded in reducing it to a simple corollary of the thought of the forgiveness of sins."[36]

However, Luther's insistence upon this "dynamic" method of referring all ethics to its source in the relationship that

. . . .

[34] W.A., 10, I, 105, 3 (Kirchenpostille, 1522, Titus 3:4-7) "Were all men to concentrate their united efforts to attain wisdom and virtue by their natural reason, knowledge, and free will—as we read, for instance, of the illustrious virtues and wisdom of certain pagan teachers and princes, Socrates, Trajan and others, to whom all the world gives written and oral applause —were all men so to do, yet such wisdom and virtue are in the sight of God nothing but sin and altogether reprehensible. The reason is, they are not attained in the grace of God." (Tr Lenker) See also W.A., 2, 408, 3 (Resolutions Concerning the Propositions Debated at Leipzig, 1519): "Virtues are distinguished by their final purpose, not by the service they render Each virtue, outside of grace, seeks its own. It cannot seek that which is God's since it is not able to do a work of love. . . Therefore no virtue has God for its final purpose nor can i

64

God establishes with man, would seem to make impossible any application of Christian ethics to those outside the Christian Church. It would seem that only those who believe in the God-man relationship which God creates through His forgiveness could be reached by the ethical demands which this relationship implies. This would indeed leave the majority of men without any valid ethical standards, and the Church without a message for the world.

However, nothing could be further from Luther's thought than to make the validity of God's will dependent upon man's subjective assent or rejection. Theology or ethics do not establish the relationship between God and man; they are for Luther merely the results of man's confrontation with God. What man thinks or says about God in theology, or does in response to God in ethical action, is merely the result of what God has done for man. Theology and ethics flow from the divine revelation as it confronts man in life, but they do not in any way condition the character of this relationship. The relationship to God shapes a man's ethics; his ethics does not shape his relationship to God.[37]

The rejection of Christianity, therefore, does not relieve

. . . .

love God above everything and for God's sake, otherwise grace would not be necessary. And this is the only reason why all the good works of the Gentiles and all natural good works are evil, since they are done without the proper final purpose." See also W.A., 2, 458, 14 ff.

[35] The term "dynamic" has been applied to Luther's method by the Swedish theologian, Gustaf Aulen. In contrast to the dialectical method of the scholastics, he calls Luther's method a "dynamic synthesis" and "unity in contrasts." Gustaf Aulen, *Den Kristna Gudsbilden,* Stockholm, 1927, p. 166.

[36] Billing, *Our Calling,* p. 7.

[37] W.A., 37, 414, 2 (Sermon on John 3:16, May 25, 1534): "You say, if God would assure me salvation personally then I would believe. But no, He has included all in His offer and I

man from the responsibility which his confrontation with God entails. Man is confronted by God all during his life through the very fact of his creatureliness and his existence within God's creation.[38] The primacy of the God-relationship makes theology and ethics not a condition of, but merely a response to, God's revelation.[39] This God-relationship of man is simply a fact of human existence and is not at all dependent upon the subjective assent of man.[40]

. . . .

must not doubt. God does not exclude anybody, but if somebody excludes himself he will have to answer for it. God says, I shall not judge them but their own mouth will judge them because they did not accept my promise."

[38] W.A., 24, 37, 24 (Sermon on Genesis, 1527): "And watch when you hear these words, 'And God said,' that these are not passing words as we speak them, but know that this is an eternal word spoken from all eternity and spoken forever. As little as God's being ever ceases, so little does His speaking ever cease, through which all creatures came into being. But God speaks still, and without pause, since no creature exists on its own. For as long as a creature exists, so long the creative word is spoken, as long as the earth bears fruit, God speaks without ceasing. . . . When we see creatures we realize there is God, because all creatures are without pause driven through His word." W.A.T., 2, 371, (2231): "Creation means not merely that God has created everything out of nothing, but also that He alone upholds everything." W.A.T., 3, 322 (3458) : "God has created everything for the sake of man. His power is so great He feeds the whole world. He has created enough of everything. The oceans are our cellars, the woods our hunting grounds, the earth is full of silver and gold and innumerable fruits, all created for our sake, so that it is our storage bin and pantry." W.A.T., 2, 232, (1833): "God could have left the world uncreated, but He created it to show His glory and power." See also W.A., 48, 214, 3 ff.

[39] W.A., 37, 412, 24 (Sermon on John 3:16, May 25, 1934): "This is what the Son does: He destroys the devil, extinguishes hell, saves me from eternal suffering. God's gift stops up hell, gives certainty and gladness to my weak heart and not only now

The will of God is valid for man whether he likes it or not, and therefore the Church has a message for all men, regardless of their religious predilections.[41]]

This is especially obvious in the realm of social ethics. What Luther has to say about the state, the family, and society in general is not based upon men's faith but is the result of the fact of their involvement in these divine orders. By the very fact of a man's calling as a father, or as a citizen,

. . . .

but forever. . . . Therefore, these (John 3:16) are words which we can never fully understand. We must pray daily that God would imprint them into our hearts. He would be a good theologian who could speak rightly of this Christ. . . . But how do I accept this gift. Where is the satchel or the case where I put this treasure? 'Whosoever believeth,' he opens his hands and his pockets. For even as God is giver through love so we are the recipients through faith. You must not try to earn it . . . your works have nothing to do with it. Let Him give it to you, keep your mouth open, hold still, and let Him give it to you."

[40] W.A., 44, 191, 19 (Comm. Genesis, 1545): "God has established the ministry of all creatures, even of the angels, in order to speed His kingdom, to sanctify His name, and that we all might be saved and inherit eternal life." W.A., 18, 80, 28 (Against the "Heavenly" Prophets, 1525): "Thou shalt not murder, commit adultery, steal, etc., is not only the law of Moses but also 'natural law' written into every heart."

[41] W.A., 16, 431, 14 (Sermon on Exodus, 1525): "But that we Gentiles also have a law is taught us by our conscience and our reason. This is also shown by St. Paul (Romans I). Here St. Paul indicates that all Gentiles have certain knowledge of God, namely that He has created everything and gives, nourishes, and maintains everything. Their own conscience tells them to give honor to God and to thank Him for all His benefits. Even if Moses never had written down the law, all men have the law by nature written in their hearts." W.A., 42, 631, 36 ff. (Comm. Genesis, 1535-45): "This knowledge the Gentiles have as a natural instinct, namely, that there is some highest being, that ought to be honored, invoked, and lauded, and to this being one can flee in all danger. . . . This knowledge God has planted into

or as a teacher, he is confronted by the God who has established certain orders for the preservation of society.[42] It is because of this involvement in the divine orders that man is at all times aware of and subject to the Divine will. His acceptance or rejection of this Divine will does not affect the reality of the confrontation with God in any way.

Here again Luther shows his interest in life, rather than in metaphysical speculation. Life confronts man with God, the creator God in the orders of nature established by Him to preserve the world, the saviour God in the Gospel of Christ which addresses man in the life-situation. Luther's

. . . .

the souls of all men and they call Him a helper, a benefactor, and gracious, although they err afterwards in establishing who this God might be and how He should be worshiped. If God is now recognized as gracious, and also that He can be propitiated, and that He does good to all men, I proceed from that and turn from Him to man and live according to my calling. If I am a ruler I take care of land and people, if I am a housefather I care for my family and servants, if I am a schoolteacher I instruct my students directing their hearts, thoughts, and deeds to the fear of God, etc. All such works are truly service to God." See also W.A., 40, I, 607, 19 ff.

methodological principle as it applies to social ethics is functional, evaluating all ethical standards in the light of the part they play in relating man to God. It is also dynamic, constantly referring all ethics to its source in the revelation of God made possible through the Gospel of the forgiveness of sins. And finally it is objective, in its application to all men. Social ethics is for Luther not the cause but the result of the confrontation of man by God. Since all men are confronted by God as His creatures living within His creation, His will was, is, and remains eternally valid for all, regardless of their subjective responses to the Divine will.

. . . .

[42] W.A., 31, I, 25 (Exp. 82nd Psalm, 1530): "Because God does not want the World to be deserted and empty, but has created it for men to dwell on and to work the land and replenish it, and since this cannot happen if there is no peace, He is forced as Creator to preserve His own creation, work, and order, and for this purpose He has established and maintains governmental authority and has given to this authority the sword and the law. This authority must kill and punish all those who disobey, since they are also opposing God's order and do not deserve life."

V. THE ETHICAL PRINCIPLE

Once the methodological principle undergirding Luther's theology, and thus also his social-ethical views, has been established, it becomes necessary to investigate more closely the specific ethical principle that underlies his social ethics. Here, too, Luther's position must be understood in relation to the contemporary situation. He did not develop his ethics in a vacuum but against the background of the scholastic ethics which dominated his age, and in very sharp contrast to this scholastic ethics. Scholastic ethics was the result of the fusion and amalgamation of biblical Christian elements with the moral philosophy of the Greek philosophers. It was an ethics dominated by Greek philosophical notions.

As soon as the Christian movement had entered the world of Hellenism, Greek thought quite naturally influenced Christianity. Such an influence could not be avoided, and was not necessarily harmful if limited to matters of form and method. In fact, much of the success of the Christian movement is attributable to the speed with which it acclimatized itself to the "Esperanto" of Hellenism and thus made its message understandable to the non-Jewish world.

However, the process of Hellenization did not stop in the

. . . .

[1] *The Ante-Nicene Fathers,* Grand Rapids, 1950-51, II, 305 (Clement of Alexandria, *The Stromata,* Book I, Chap. 5): "Accordingly, before the advent of the Lord, philosophy was necessary to the Greeks for righteousness. . . . Perchance, too, philosophy was given to the Greeks directly and primarily, till the Lord should call the Greeks. For this was a schoolmaster to bring the Hellenic mind, as the law, the Hebrews, to Christ. Philosophy, therefore, was a preparation paving the way for him who is perfected in Christ." Cf. II, 489, *The Stromata,* Book VI, Chap. 5: "For clearly, as I think, he showed that the one and only God was known by the Greeks in a Gentile way, by the Jews Judaically, and in a new and spiritual way by us. And

realm of method but affected the content of the Christian message as well. The influence of Greek ideas became especially strong in the field of ethics, where contemporary philosophic notions of virtue and goodness were incorporated, almost without alteration, into the developing system of Christian ethics. In their apologetic efforts the early Christian theologians tended to minimize the very real differences that existed between the Christian "life in Christ" and the "virtue" of pagan philosophy. Clement of Alexandria, for example, considered Greek philosophical and moral teachings the equivalent of the Old Testament, and preparatory revelations of the Divine Logos.[1] He understood ethics in such a predominantly philosophical manner that only God remained worthy of "ethical" love, and as a result the biblical emphasis upon the concrete love to the neighbor was quite naturally pushed into the background.[2]

Similarly, Origen, in his efforts to fuse Greek and Christian notions, brought about a synthesis between Greek philosophical morality, based upon man's striving for happiness, and the Christian life of fellowship with Christ.[3] Thus, genuinely Christian ethical ideas were consistently interpreted in terms of Greek philosophy.

Although Origen was eventually declared a heretic, his paganization of Christian ethics prevailed. Even Augustine, who fought valiantly against the conquest of Christianity

. . . .

further, that the same God that furnished both the Covenants was the giver of Greek philosophy to the Greeks, by which the Almighty is glorified by the Greeks." See also the discussion of this subject in Anders Nygren, *Agape and Eros,* London, 1932-39, Part II, Vol. I, 138.

[2] Ibid., 133 ff.

[3] Ibid., 152 ff. When comparing the most profound insights of Plato and the deepest insights of Christianity, it appears to Origen that Christianity's chief advantage is its greater simplicity. Cf. *Ante-Nicene Fathers,* IV, 573 (Origen against Celsus, Book VI, Chap. 2).

by paganism when he opposed Pelagius, and who achieved a temporary triumph in the field of dogmatics when the Church condemned Pelagianism at the General Synod of Carthage, left the door wide open to the disintegrating influences of paganism in the field of ethics. In fact, it was Augustine who placed the weight of his authority behind a neo-platonic and eudaimonistic conception of love which assured Greek philosophical ethics a dominating position in Christian ethical thought for the next thousand years.[4]

However, in Augustine's thought the purely Christian elements always outweighed the very noticeable pagan and neo-platonic influence. It was left to Thomas Aquinas to construct a synthesis of Greek philosophy and Christian faith which neatly balanced both elements. For Aquinas, Christian ethics was no longer the result of the fellowship which God establishes with man and which St. Paul described when he said, "It is no longer I that live, but Christ liveth in me; and that life which I now live in the flesh I live in faith, the faith which is in the Son of God who loved me and gave himself for me." (Gal. 2:20) For Aquinas,

. . . .

[4] Nygren, II, II, 231 ff. See also Holl, *Gesammelte Aufsätze,* I, 161 ff. and III, 107 ff. Switalski, who discusses the influence of Plotinus upon Augustine from the Roman Catholic point of view, says: "It is then evident that Augustine does not blindly follow the Neo-platonic philosopher but judges his doctrine in the light of the authority of the Church . . . and that he selected only those ideas from the writings of Plotinus which were not opposed to Christian revelation." Yet he also states: "Either as wholly or at least partially consistent with the teachings of the Church, Augustine regards the following: supreme happiness, its concrete object, i.e., the vision of God, the way leading to God, the problem of evil and the doctrine of the eternal law." (Bruno Switalski, *Neo-platonism and the Ethics of St. Augustine,* Polish Institute of Arts and Sciences in America, New York, 1946, I, 107, 109) It is exactly Augustine's tendency to regard these matters as presented by Plotinus as consistent with the teachings of the Church, which have led Holl and Nygren to accuse him

Christian ethics was not the road of life in fellowship with God, but rather the road leading to fellowship with God. The idea which dominates scholastic ethics is contained in the words of Aquinas: "Man obtains happiness by many movements of works which are called merits."[5] Although Aquinas denied the possibility that man could reach this blessedness unaided by Divine grace, he nevertheless considered ethics the result of the cooperation between Divine grace and human merit. According to scholasticism, "Man can reach beatitude only by merit."[6] Thus merit became the ethical principle that dominated scholastic theology. Under the influence of the Greek philosophers the egocentric striving for merits became the motivating force of the Christian life.

The great theological systems of the scholastics had been challenged before Luther's time by the nominalists. The leaders of the nominalistic revolution against Thomism felt that the combination of Hellenism and Christianity, philosophy and theology, Aristotle and St. Paul, could at best camouflage the issues and produce an uneasy armistice. For this

. . . .

of perverting Christian ethics.

[5] *The Summa Theologica of St. Thomas Aquinas,* trans. by Fathers of the English Dominican Province, London, 1920, Part II, 1, Qu. 5, Art. 7 (VI, 82): "Now to possess the perfect good without movement belongs to that which has it naturally: and to have Happiness naturally belongs to God alone. Therefore it belongs to God alone not to be moved towards Happiness by any previous operation. Now since Happiness surpasses every created nature, no pure creature can becomingly gain Happiness without the movement of operation, whereby it tends thereto. But the angel who is above man in the natural order obtained it according to the order of Divine wisdom, by one movement of a meritorious work, as was explained in the First Part; whereas man obtains it by many movements of works which are called merits. Wherefore also according to the Philosopher (Ethics I, 9) happiness is the reward of works of virtue."

reason they rejected the Thomistic synthesis. But the attack of the nominalists against Aquinas was essentially a philosophical attack against the philosophical claims of Thomism rather than a religious attack against its religious assertions. William of Ockham, for example, attacked Aquinas' philosophical proofs for the existence of God, as well as his proofs for the existence of a thinking soul, because he considered them poor philosophy, not because they were poor Christianity.[7] This merely confused the basic issue. Luther was aware of the confusion that philosophy had caused within the theology whose handmaid it was alleged to be. He realized that the handmaid had actually usurped the throne of the queen. He knew also that philosophy would have to be dethroned if theology was ever again to serve the Church of Christ. As a student at the University of Erfurt, where nominalism reigned, and particularly through the writings of Gabriel Biel,[8] Luther had become quite familiar with

. . . .

[6] Ibid., I, Qu. 62, Art. 4, (III, 131).

[7] Cf. Walter Betzendörfer, *Glauben und Wissen bei den Grossen Denkern des Mittelalters,* Gotha, 1931 p. 243. "According to Ockham it is impossible to prove the existence of God. The alleged proofs for God's existence are not proofs properly speaking; at best they contain an element of probability. It is thinkable that the world might exist of itself and move itself. It is impossible to prove from natural reason that God is the immediate cause of all things for it is sufficiently demonstrable that other causes, as for example heavenly bodies, are sufficient to explain many effects. Furthermore, it is impossible to prove from natural reason that God is the effective cause of any effect. . . . It also cannot be proved that the intelligent soul (anima intellectiva) was caused by an effective cause, for it is impossible to demonstrate that such a soul exists in us."

[8] The following references to Gabriel Biel in Luther's *Table-Talk* throw some light on his later attitude towards these theologians. W.A.T., 3, 192 (3146): "One must not forget what the papists have done. They must be uncovered because they are now trying to cover their deeds and act as if they had never

the theological controversies that had disturbed the Christian faith for centuries.[9] The nominalists taught him to suspect the scholastic synthesis of philosophy and theology, yet at the same time Luther rejected the nominalistic escape into the arbitrary and absolute authority of the church. To him only a theology free from the fetters of pagan philosophy would prove an effective servant of the church.

But Luther had seen the most dangerous results of the amalgamation of paganism and Christianity in the field of ethics. Following Aristotle, scholasticism had emphasized the natural abilities of man to live the virtuous life. Luther realized that it was this emphasis upon man's ability rather than God's grace which was at the bottom of the eudaimonistic perversion of ethics under the papacy.[10] It was Aristotle who had held that God loves Himself only and because of His very perfection could not consider anything but Himself. He had said: "It must be of itself that the divine

. . . .

troubled the waters. Thus young people, who do not remember their blasphemies and idolatries, are easily led astray. The papists must be put to shame with their own works, examples, and teachings. Take only Gabriel Biel, *On the Canon of the Mass,* which is the best book of the papists—and yet what awful things it contains. At one time this was my favorite book." W.A.T., 3, 564, 5 (3722): "Gabriel (Biel) wrote a book on the Canon of the Mass, which book seemed to me at the time the very best; whenever I read it my heart would bleed. The authority of the Bible was nothing compared with Gabriel. I still have these books that tortured me so much."

[9] Cf. Boehmer, *Road to Reformation,* pp. 44 ff.

[10] W.A., 7, 739, 19 (Luther's Reply to M. Ambrosius Catharinus, 1521): " 'And they had a king, an angel from the abyss whose name was in Hebrew Abbadon, in Greek Apollyon.'—Here we hear who is the highest ruler over all universities, not Christ, not the Holy Spirit, not an angel of the Lord, but the angel from the abyss, i.e., one who is dead, and from the dead and damned. Who is he? That great light of nature even Aristotle, who is truly an Apollyon, a destroyer and wrecker of the Church, he

thought thinks (since it is the most excellent of things), and its thinking is a thinking on thinking."[11] This had given his authority to the egocentric motivation of ethics, so clearly part of scholastic theology.[12] Christian ethics, in order to again become truly Christian, had to be freed from philosophical ethics. As early as 1514, Luther complained about the influence of Aristotle on Christian thinking. Later, in September, 1517, one of his students, Franz Günther, publicly defended ninety-seven theses against the "Scholastic Theology," which brought approval in Wittenberg but concern and criticism from Luther's alma mater, the University of Erfurt. But Luther and his friends realized that it was impossible to reform the Church without opposing Aristotle and his scholastic disciples who had laid the foundation for the paganization of Christianity. In the disputation against the "Scholastic Theology" the following opinions were openly attacked: "39. We are not masters of our actions from beginning to end, but servants—against the philosophers. 40. We do not become righteous by doing righteous

. . . .

rules now in our universities. Though he was not worthy to be named by name in Holy Scripture. . . . And it is certain that this dead and condemned Aristotle is today the teacher at all our universities, more so than Christ. He rules, elevated to this position through the authority and industry of Thomas (Aquinas), and he has revived 'free will,' and teaches us moral virtues and natural philosophy. . . ."

[11] *The Student's Oxford Aristotle,* ed. W. D. Ross, London, 1942, IV, Metaphysics, 1074 b, 32 (Met. XI, 9).

[12] W.A., 40, III, 322, 16 (Psalm 129:4, 1532-35):". . . just as Aristotle accepts the proposition that God, though he does not call Him stupid, remains ignorant of all things. He does not see or understand our affairs and considers nothing but Himself and enjoys Himself speculating about His own self." W.A., 20, 612, 37 ff. (Exp., I John 1:5, 1527): "Aristotle reasons as follows: If God saw everything that occurs here He would never have a quiet mind, therefore He does not observe us."

works, but being made righteous we do righteous works—against the philosophers. 41. Almost the entire ethics of Aristotle is the worst enemy of grace—against the scholastics. 42. It is an error to claim that Aristotle's propositions on happiness are not repugnant to catholic doctrine—against the moral theologians. 43. It is an error to insist that without Aristotle one cannot become a theologian—against common opinion. 44. Indeed, no one becomes a theologian if not without Aristotle. . . . 50. In short, all of Aristotle is to theology what darkness is to light."[13] Luther complained that philosophical ethics spoke always of our natural light, our reason, our free will, our natural powers.[14] Against such an emphasis upon the human abilities, a theological ethics had to stress the all-importance of faith for Christian conduct. Luther said:

> "The first and highest, the most precious of all good works is faith in Christ, as He says, John 6. When the Jews asked Him: 'What shall we do that

. . . .

[13] W.A., 1, 221 ff. (Disputation Against the Scholastic Theology, 1517).

[14] W.A., 17, II, 27, 25 (Fastenpostille, 1525): "As we have said above (W.A., 10, I, 1, 584 ff.), they filled the world with three kinds of teachings which led people away from the Word of God. The first is the very crude teaching of St. Thomas and other scholastics, which is the result of pagan art and natural reason. Of this they said that the light of nature is a beautiful clear table and Scripture is the sun shining on this table and making it glitter even more beautifully. Thus the Divine light shines upon the light of nature and enlightens it. With this parable they injected pagan teaching into Christianity and this pagan teaching dominated the universities so that eventually the parable became reversed and they tried to use the art of reason and of Aristotle to enlighten Scripture, which indeed is the only true light without which all the light of reason is absolute darkness as far as Divine matters and articles of faith are concerned."

we may work the works of God?' He answered: 'This is the work of God, that ye believe on Him Whom He hath sent.' When we hear or preach this word, we hasten over it and deem it a very little thing and easy to do, whereas we ought here to pause a long time to ponder it well. For in this work all good works must be done and receive from it the inflow of their goodness, like a loan. We find many who pray, fast, establish endowments, do this or that, lead a good life before men, and yet if you should ask them whether they are sure that what they do pleases God, they say, 'No'; they do not know, or they doubt. And there are some very learned men, who mislead them, and say that it is not necessary to be sure of this; and yet, on the other hand, these same men do nothing else but teach good works. Now all these works are done outside of faith, therefore they are nothing and altogether dead. For as their conscience stands

· ·

[15] Phila. Ed., I, 187 ff. (Treatise on Good Works).

[16] It seems that Luther felt very clearly that Aristotle's claim that moral virtue is an acquired skill was at the bottom of the scholastics' emphasis upon merits and caused them to believe that an evil man could become good by merely doing good works. Aristotle said in his *Nicomachean Ethics:* "Again, of all the things that come to us by nature we first acquire the potentiality and later exhibit the activity; but the virtues we get by first exercising them, as also the things we have to learn before we can do them we learn by doing them. E.g., men become builders by building and lyre-players by playing the lyre; so too we become just by doing just acts, temperate by doing temperate acts, brave by doing brave acts." *(The Student's Oxford Aristotle,* V, 1103 a) This was Luther's reaction: "For he is not righteous who acts righteously, as Aristotle says, and we are not called righteous when doing righteous deeds, but when we believe and trust in God." (W.A., 1, 84, 19 ff, Sermon, August 24, 1516.)

toward God and as it believes, so also are the works which grow out of it."[15]

For Luther only faith could guarantee ethical action.

It is small wonder that from this vantage point Luther criticized Aristotle bitterly.[16] This was not an attack against philosophy as such and in its own sphere. There are indications that Luther appreciated certain writings of Aristotle,[17] and in his commentary on Galatians he stated that the trouble with Aristotle was mainly the false application of his philosophical insights to matters of Christian theology. He said: "Therefore is such a pagan philosopher much better than a hypocritical advocate of work-righteousness. For he realized his limitations and concerned himself with honesty and civil tranquillity and did not mix the Divine and the human."[18] This attempt to build theology on the foundation of philosophy Luther rejected firmly. He expressed his feeling clearly in one of his table-talks when he said: "Human reason can go no further with all its wisdom than to teach people how they shall govern themselves and live

. . . .

[17] Luther appreciated particularly Aristotle's *Logic, Rhetoric, Poetry* (W.A., 6, 458, 26), and the fifth book of the *Ethics* (W.A., 44, 704, 15), but occasionally he commented favorably even on Aristotle's *Physics, Metaphysics,* and *De Anima* (W.A.T., 1, 57, 41). It seemed to Luther that one of the main reasons for Aristotle's bad influence on theology was the misunderstanding of his philosophy by the scholastics. This applied particularly to the injection of the substance-accident terminology into the discussion of the sacrament of Holy Communion. He said in his treatise on *The Babylonian Captivity of the Church* (1520): "For Aristotle treats so very different from St. Thomas of subject and accidents, that methinks this great man is to be pitied, not only for drawing his opinions in matters of faith from Aristotle, but for attempting to base them on him without understanding his meaning—an unfortunate superstructure upon an unfortunate foundation." (Phila. Ed., II, 188 ff.)

[18] W.A., 40, I, 17 ff.

79

honestly in this temporal and passing life, what they have to do to be respected in this world, and leave that which causes trouble and is not becoming to them. But how one can know our Lord God and His dear Son Jesus Christ and how one is saved—that the Holy Spirit alone teaches through the Word of God. And I am afraid they will again mix philosophy with theology, although I do not have any objections to the teaching and study of philosophy. In fact I laud and approve it, but it must be done with modesty; one must leave philosophy in its circle where God has placed it."[19]

Through the efforts of the scholastics, philosophy not only ruled in its own field but also dominated Christian teaching. This was a situation which Luther considered intolerable, especially since the influence of Aristotle tended to cultivate work-righteousness. It was Aristotle who, according to Luther, had taught that he who does many good works will in this manner become good. This seemed to him a complete perversion of Christian ethics.[20] According to Luther, the main difference between philosophical and theological ethics consists in the fact that the one stresses man's work and the other stresses God's work. Philosophical ethics can therefore never be Christian ethics since it starts from the wrong presupposition. Of course, Luther was aware of the fact that grace is not excluded in the scholastic synthesis. But the idea of a free will that cooperates with the grace of God, as held by the scholastics, and as developed against him by Erasmus,

. . . .

[19] W.A.T., 5, 25, 24 ff. (5245).

[20] W.A., 10, I, 326 (Kirchenpostille): "Hence the natural man can perform no good work, and all his attempts will be no better than Cain's. Here Madam Huldah with her scornful nose—human nature—steps in, dares to contradict her God and to charge him with falsehood. She hangs upon herself her old frippery, her straw armor—natural light, reason, free will and human powers. She introduces the heathenish books and doctrines of men, and proceeds to harp upon these saying: "Good

80

seemed to Luther a betrayal of justification by faith.

Luther objected also to the eudaimonistic tendencies of scholastic ethics. He realized that under the influence of Greek philosophy, scholasticism had developed an ethical system based on the human striving for happiness. In order to obtain this eternal happiness it was advisable for man to practice self-denial. The value of a good work was then measured by the amount of self-denial it implied.[21] Scholastic ethics was ultimately concerned with the happiness of the ethical individual, and ethical action was evaluated by the temporal unhappiness it caused him. As a result of the influence of Aristotle and Greek philosophy in general, the ethical system of scholasticism was egocentric and anthropocentric.

This became obvious in the casuistic dissolution of the absolute demands of God into commands and counsels. Thomas Aquinas put it like this: "The difference between a counsel and a commandment is that a commandment implies obligation, whereas a counsel is left to the option of the one to whom it is given. Consequently, in the New Law, which is the law of liberty, counsels are added to the commandments, and not in the Old Law, which is the law of bondage. We must therefore understand the commandments of the New Law to have been given about matters that are necessary to gain the end of eternal bliss, to which end the New Law brings us forthwith: but the counsels are about matters that render the gaining of this end more

. . . .

works do precede justification. And they are not as God says, the works of Cain. They are good to the extent of justifying. For Aristotle taught that he who does much good will thereby become good." (Tr. Lenker)

[21] This is indicated as early as the Second Letter of Clement, (16:4): "Almsgiving is therefore good even as penitence for sin; fasting is better than prayer; but the giving of alms is better than both." (*The Apostolic Fathers,* Cambridge, 1912, I, 155.) See also Holl, op.cit., I, 162, note 4.

assured and expeditious."[22] Aquinas declared that in order to attain eternal blessedness it is not necessary to renounce the things of the world altogether. Man can, "while using the things of this world, attain to eternal happiness, provided he does not place his end in them; but he will attain more speedily thereto by giving up the goods of this world entirely: wherefore the evangelical counsels are given for this purpose."[23]

The scholastic theologians made a valiant effort for the sake of greater rationality to make obedience to the divine commands a simple human possibility. This could not be done without practically rewriting large sections of the Bible where these harsh demands of God could be found. But rather than renounce philosophy in the field of Christian ethics, the scholastic theologians re-interpreted the Bible in terms of Aristotelian ethics. Thus the command to love God with all the heart and soul was declared not binding for this life.[24]

At the same time the love for the neighbor was also "simplified." This love was interpreted by the official Roman theologians as being based upon self-love.[25] Furthermore, the concept of the neighbor was so interpreted as to mean those who are naturally closest to the person called to love.

. . . .

[22] Aquinas, *Summa Theologica*, II, 1, Qu. 108, Art. 4 (VIII, 317).

[23] Ibid., VIII, 318.

[24] Ibid., II, 2, Qu. 24, Art. 9 (IX, 294): "On the part of the person who loves, charity is perfect, when he loves as much as he can. This happens in three ways. First, so that a man's whole heart is always actually borne towards God: this is the perfection of the charity of heaven, and is not possible in this life, wherein, by reason of the weakness of human life, it is impossible to think always actually of God, and to be moved by love towards Him. Secondly, so that man makes an earnest endeavour to give his time to God and Divine things, while scorning other things except in so far as the needs of the present life demand. This

82

In this manner the non-prudential character of the love commandment was rationalistically dissolved.[26]

To Luther all this seemed the result of the great influence of philosophical speculation upon ethics. By means of philosophy and the "right" use of reason the absolute commands of God had been made workable and practical; however, they were no longer absolute commands of God and a revelation of His own Divine Love, but merely reasonable suggestions and counsels. Against all these perversions of Christian ethics in scholasticism and the official Roman theology Luther placed his theological ethics.

Luther's ethics received its basic principle not from philosophy but from the Word of God. It was a "theological" or "evangelical" ethics based upon the witness of the Gospel. Its basic principle was consequently quite different from all the accepted assumptions of philosophical ethics. Starting with revelation instead of reason, it denied the heretofore sacred assumption of the Christian character of ordered self-love and neglected altogether the motive of all philosophical ethics, namely the desire for happiness. Completely disregarding the secret hedonism and the religious profit-motive of the official Roman theologians, Luther suggested an entirely different basic motive for Christian action. Luther

. . . .

is the perfection of charity that is possible to a wayfarer; but it is not common to all who have charity. Thirdly, so that a man gives his whole heart to God habitually, viz. by neither thinking nor desiring anything contrary to the love of God; and this perfection is common to all who have charity."

[25] Ibid., II, 1, Qu. 77, Art. 4 (VII, 366): "Well-ordered self-love, whereby man desires a fitting good for himself, is right and natural."

[26] Ibid., II, 2, Qu. 44, Art. 8 (IX, 552): "When we are commanded (Gal. 6:10) to work good . . . especially to those who are of the household of the faith . . . it means that we ought to love most those of our neighbors who are more virtuous or more closely united to us. Reply Obj. 3. It follows from the very

took this new principle directly from the Bible, yet it seemed to his contemporaries as if he had discovered something completely new.

Luther said that justification is the basis for all Christian ethics. There is no Christian ethics apart from Christian people; and only people justified by faith are Christian people.[27] It was Luther who insisted that the person precedes the act, that ethics is always the ethics of people, and that one cannot have moral acts apart from moral people. He expressed this thought repeatedly in his book *On Christian Liberty*. Here he said: "Good works do not make a good man, but a good man does good works; evil works do not make a wicked man, but a wicked man does evil works; so

. . . .

words, 'Thou shalt love thy neighbour,' that those who are nearer to us are to be loved more."

[27] W.A., 17, II, 166, 15 (Fastenpostille, 1525, I Cor. 13:1 ff.): "Justification of necessity precedes love. One does not love until he has become godly and righteous. Love does not make us godly, but when one has become godly love is the result. Faith, the Spirit, and justification have love as effect and fruitage, and not as a mere ornament and supplement. We maintain that faith alone justifies and saves." (Tr. Lenker) See also W.A., 17, II, 97 29 (Fastenpostille, Romans 13:8 ff.): "On the other hand, love and works do not change us, do not justify us. We must be changed in person and justified before we can love and do good works. Our love and our works are evidence of justification and of a change, since they are impossible until the individual is free from sin and made righteous. . . . Just as the law in requiring works before faith exists is a sign to the individual leading him to recognize his utter lack of faith and righteousness, and to conclude he is conquered, so love in its fulfillment of the law after faith intervenes is a sign and a proof to the individual of his faith and righteousness."

[28] Phila. Ed., II, 331; cf. W.A., 32, 520, 10 (Exp. Matthew 7:16-20, 1530-32): "But as little as I can see in my calling that my fruit is good, as little can the other person [monk] see that his calling is worthless and useless. They can therefore turn this word around and say that a bad tree brings forth good

that it is always necessary that the 'substance' or person itself be good before there can be any good works, and that good follow and proceed from the good person, as Christ also says, 'A corrupt tree does not bring forth good fruit, a good tree does not bring forth evil fruit.' "[28]

But how does man become pious and a Christian in Luther's sense of the word? From what moment on are his works good works? The justification which makes man just in the eyes of God and a doer of good works is a free gift.[29] It is a foreign gift that comes to us from the outside.[30] It is sanctity appropriated by faith in the Word of God promising forgiveness of sins. Faith is never unethical faith. He who has faith will be sanctified and do good works. Justification

. . . .

fruits and a good tree brings forth evil fruits. This means that reason cannot judge and see the goodness of a calling and of its works and does not enjoy it and have pleasure from it. On the contrary, reason will praise the opposite. For if we could only see it we would all rejoice in our callings and suffer gladly what God has put upon us, knowing that since the tree is good the fruits must also be good. Thus a godly hired man when he hauls a load of manure to the field is carrying a load of the most precious figs and grapes—but in the eyes of God and not in our eyes who do not believe and therefore despise each our own calling and covet something else."

[29] W.A., 39, I, 129, 12 (Disputation on Luke 7:47, 1535): "The second is the other word of Christ, 'To whom little is forgiven, the same loveth little.' With these words He indicates that the forgiveness of sins comes before love, and the latter follows the forgiveness of sins as gratitude for a gift received. For He does not say here, 'Him, who loveth little, little will be forgiven,' but on the contrary, 'He loveth little to whom little is forgiven.' This shows clearly that forgiveness is free and received without merit, but love is the fruit and confession of the donated forgiveness."
[30] W.A., 40, II, 352, 33 (Comm. Psalm 51, 1532): "A Christian who has been justified by faith and received the forgiveness of sins must not be so secure as if he were totally free from all sins. For now it is up to him to fight constantly against the remnants of sin (from which the prophet here desires to be

and sanctification are for Luther two aspects of the same process and therefore mutually interdependent.[31]

According to Luther it is quite incorrect to describe justification as the work of God and sanctification as the response of man, as if man could be justified without being sanctified. On the contrary, "Holy are as many as believe in Christ, be they men or women, slaves or free, etc., not because of their own works but because of the work of God which they receive in faith, as there are the Word, Sacraments, Christ's suffering, death and resurrection, victory, outpouring of the Holy Spirit, etc."[32]

Although Luther had excluded all human merit in his explanation of the motivating principle of Christian ethics,

. . . .

washed). The Christian is just and holy through a foreign and extrinsic holiness (as a teacher I am using the technical term) that means he is just through the mercy and grace of God. This mercy and grace is not something human, it is not a 'habit' or a 'quality' of the heart, but it is a Divine favor, given to us through the proper recognition of the Gospel, namely that we know and believe that our sin has been forgiven through Christ's grace and merit. For Christ's sake we can hope for mercy and much and great pity, as the prophet here said. But isn't this justice a foreign justice? It consists entirely in the remission by somebody else and is a clear gift of God who has pity and favors us for Christ's sake."

[31] W.A., 45, 703, 1 (Exp. John 15, 1537): "Indeed, you say, but does not faith justify and save without works? Certainly this is true, but where is this faith, where does it remain? How does it prove itself? For it cannot be a lazy, useless, deaf and dead thing but must be a living fruitful tree bursting with fruits. This is therefore the distinction and proof dividing true faith and false or counterfeit faith—where faith is true it shows itself in life, but the false faith uses the same name, word, and fame, but has no result." See also W.A., 12, 289, 28 (Exp. I Peter, 1523): "When the Apostle says here that God judgeth us according to our works it is certainly true. But one must also keep in mind that where there is no faith there cannot be any good work, and again that there is no faith wherever good works fail

he did not want to imply that this was to exclude good works from the Christian life. Christians were to be free from good works only if these works were understood as producing "work-righteousness." On the other hand, Luther insisted that a living faith expresses itself in works of love. These good works, however, follow spontaneously and not under the compulsion of the law. And although the law itself does not change, the Christian's attitude towards the law is so utterly changed by faith that he becomes a lover of the law instead of being merely its slave. The works of the law are not forced out of him against his will but are the free expression of his new faith.[33] Real faith "is a divine work in us. It changes us and makes us to be born anew of God; it kills

. . . .

to be found. Therefore faith and good works must be put together so that in both together the total Christian life is contained. As you live, so you will be treated; in this manner God will judge you. But though God judges us according to our works, it remains true that the works are purely fruits of faith which show where there is faith and where there is unbelief. God will judge you and convince you from your works and show you whether you believed or didn't. Just as it is impossible to judge a liar except by his words, yet it is obvious that his words do not make him a liar but that he was a liar before he ever uttered a lie, for lies come from the heart into the mouth. Now understand this word simply thus: The works are fruits and signs of faith and God judges men according to these fruits which must of necessity follow, so that one can see publicly where there is faith and where there is unbelief in the heart. God will not judge you according to your title 'Christian' or by your baptism, but He will ask you, 'If you are a Christian, tell me, where are the fruits which prove your faith?' "

[32] W.A., 5, 58 (Works on the Psalms, 1519-20, Psalm 2:6): "That is holy which has been separated from profane use and dedicated to sacred and Divine uses only. This is done ceremonially and literally through men, the bishops, but it is done in truth and in the Spirit through the Holy Spirit who is poured into our hearts."

[33] W.A., 2, 560, 21 (Comm. Gal. 5:1, 1519): "Human liberty

the old Adam, and makes altogether different men, in heart and spirit and mind and powers, and it brings with it the Holy Ghost. O, it is a living, busy, active, mighty thing, this faith; and so it is impossible for it not to do good works incessantly. It does not ask whether there are good works to do, but before the question arises it has already done them, and is always at the doing of them."[34] Faith is always active in love.[35] Luther found support for this view in his study of St. Paul's Epistle to the Galatians and particularly in the sixth verse of the fifth chapter, "For in Christ Jesus neither circumcision nor uncircumcision is of any avail, but faith working through love." Luther said that the Apostle teaches plainly that faith must be active in love. Love is the tool of faith, the instrument through which faith deals with the fellow man. It is through love that faith accomplishes its works. But, Luther continued, everybody knows that a tool has no power of itself but receives its power from the laborer who wields it. It is therefore foolish to say that the ax gives the carpenter the strength to cut. But to say that love is the

. . . .

means to change the laws without changing men. Christian liberty means that men are changed without changing the law, so that the very same law, which was previously hated by the free will is now made pleasant because love has been poured into our hearts through the Holy Spirit. He teaches that we should stand courageously and firmly in this liberty since Christ, fulfilling the law for us and overcoming our sin, sends the spirit of love into the hearts of those who believe in Him. And through this work of Christ they become righteous and lovers of the law, not, indeed, through their own works but because of the generosity of Christ through grace."

[34] Phila. Ed., VI, 451 ff. (Preface to Romans).

[35] To the following see W.A., 40, II, 34, 8 ff. (Comm. Gal., 1531).

[36] W.A., 40, II, 37, 15 (Comm. Gal.): "He who wants to be a true Christian and in Christ's kingdom must be truly a believer. And he does not truly believe if works of love do not follow his

essential character of faith or supplies its strength to faith is equally foolish. He who truly desires to be a Christian must be a truly believing man. A person whose faith is barren and not followed by works of love does not truly believe.

The Christian life is indeed a life of faith and love, but faith is the Christian's attitude towards God, and love is the Christian's attitude towards his fellow man which follows from faith. Faith in God through Christ is the necessary presupposition for love to our fellow man, and it is therefore the source of all ethics.[36]

This new basis for ethical action, faith active in love, sounds at first very similar to the Roman conception of faith formed by love *(fides caritate formata);* however, Luther explained the difference fully and in detail. Human love does not and cannot form faith; on the contrary, all true Christian love is the result of the creative activity of faith. "Faith does not rest but serves the neighbor in love"—that is Luther's conviction which is at the basis of all his utterances about the relationship between faith and works, dog-

. . . .

faith. And so Paul excludes on both sides, the right and the left, the hypocrites from Christ's kingdom. On the left he excludes the Jews and those who rely on their works. Here, he says, before Christ neither circumcision, i.e., works, nor worship, nor any other condition of life, but only faith without any trust in works, has any validity. On the right he excludes those who are idle, lazy, and indolent, who say: If faith justifies without works, we won't do any works but only 'believe' and then do as we please. Not so, you godless people, says Paul. It is true that we are justified by faith alone without works, but I speak of the true faith which after it justifies does not snore lazily, but is active in love. Thus, as I have said, Paul depicts here the entire Christian life, showing that faith is directed internally towards God, love and works are directed externally towards the neighbor. And a man is wholly Christian if he is it internally through faith before God (who does not need our works) and externally before men (who are not helped by our faith) through works and love."

89

matics and ethics.[37] Luther substituted for the Roman slogan of "faith formed by love" the biblical word "faith forming love" or "faith active in love" (Gal. 5:6). Thus, if the principle of Luther's ethics can be defined in relation to its source in God as "justification by faith," it can be described in relation to its outlet as "faith active in love."[38]

These statements of Luther must not be understood in a perfectionist sense. Luther was free from any illusions in regard to the perfection that man could possibly achieve in this life. He did not believe that after their experience of justification men would be immediately and completely free from sin. On the contrary, he always spoke of Christians as righteous and sinners at the same time. In his commentary on St. Paul's Epistle to the Romans he said, "Remarkable is God in His saints. Before Him they are at the same time righteous and unrighteous. And He is remarkable in the hypocrites. Before Him they are at the same time unright-

. . . .

[37] E.A., 52, 158: "We have frequently said that although man is justified by faith and owns Christ without the help of works, yet works are not left behind but follow with certainty. For faith does not rest but serves the neighbor through love and contends with the other sins and lusts in the flesh until death."

[38] W.A., 40, I, 275, 12 (Comm. Gal., 1531) : "Afterwards, when I have apprehended Christ in faith and have died to the law and have been justified from sin and freed from death, devil, and hell through Christ—then I do good works, love God, give thanks and show love to the neighbor. But this love or the resulting works do not "form my faith" nor do they decorate it, but my faith forms and decorates love. This is our theology and as far as reason is concerned it may appear paradoxical (para-doxa), astonishing, and absurd (absurda) that as far as the law is concerned I am not only blind and deaf and free of it but also completely dead unto it."

[39] W.A., 56, 269, 21 ff. (Comm. Romans, 1515-16).

[40] Jacobs, Book of Concord, p. 474 (The Large Catechism): "Finally, we must also know what baptism signifies, and why

eous and righteous. Since the saints have their own sin always before their eyes and ask for God's justice according to His mercy, therefore God considers them always righteous. Thus, they are in their own eyes and in reality unrighteous, but before God, who because of their confession of sins considers them righteous, they are righteous. In reality they are sinners but they are righteous in the sight of the merciful God. Without knowing it, they are righteous; according to their knowledge they are unrighteous. Sinners in reality, they are righteous in hope."[39]

But this again does not mean that sin is something static in God's saints and not in any way affected or changed by the fact of justification and sanctification. On the contrary, there must be a development in the Christian life; the Old Adam must decrease and the New Adam must increase.[40] The freedom from the law is valid only for the New Adam, and as far as man is ruled by the New Adam. Luther asserted

. . . .

God has ordained just such external sign and form for the sacrament by which we are first received into the Christian Church. But the act or form is this, that we are sunk under the water, which passes over us, and afterwards are drawn out again. These two parts, to be sunk under the water and drawn out again signify the power and efficacy of baptism, which is nothing else than putting to death the Old Adam, and after that the resurrection of the new man, both of which must take place in us all our lives. So that a truly Christian life is nothing else than a daily baptism, once begun and ever to be continued. For this must be practiced without ceasing, that we ever keep purging away whatever is of the Old Adam, and that that which belongs to the new man may come forth. But what is the old man? It is that which is born in us from Adam, malicious, hateful, envious, lascivious, avaricious, indolent, haughty, yea, unbelieving, infected with all vices and having by nature nothing good in it. When now we are received into the kingdom of Christ, these things must daily decrease, that we daily become more gentle, more patient, more meek, and ever withdrawn more and more from unbelief, avarice, hatred, envy, haughtiness."

that man needs the law as a check for the Old Adam: "If you need the law," he wrote, "you need it for the flesh and the Old Adam, to keep him orderly and in obedience to the Ten Commandments of God. But your faith, your heart, and your conscience must be free of the law, and the law in your heart must melt before the name 'eternal father' as ice melts in the heat of summer."[41]

Of course, it is impossible for man to separate the Old Adam clearly and neatly from the new. Man cannot say, here I am righteous and the New Adam is active and here I am unrighteous and the Old Adam is active. Such a procedure would demand a split personality. Luther realized that and said in his commentary on Romans: "One and the same man is spiritual and carnal, righteous and sinful, good and evil."[42] "And the just man is like a rusty tool, which God began to polish, but which, where it is rusty, does not cut until it is perfectly polished."[43] This process of polishing goes on as long as man lives.[44] But it is God who does the polishing: that is the important difference between Luther's ethics and the ethics of Rome.

. . . .

[41] E.A., 6, 302 (Sermon, St. John's Day, 1531). See also W.A., 31, I, 419 (Comm. Psalm 111, 1530): "God pounds and works on us, planing and carving, in order to kill the old man in us and all his wisdom, intelligence, and holiness, indeed, with all his vices. In this way He prepares us perfectly to become His new creatures. But He has to use mighty axes and hatchets, saws and wedges (for the Old Adam is a tough old hide), i.e., evil tyrants, devil, anarchists, false brethren, hunger, pestilence, sickness, prison, rope, and sword. Who can count them all? This work lasts until death."

[42] W.A., 56, 343, 18 (Comm. Romans, 1515-16).

[43] W.A., 2, 413, 27.

[44] W.A., 36, 364, 19 (Sermon on I Tim., Nov. 24, 1532): "For as I have said, even if I have a clear conscience before men and show love from a pure heart, the Old Adam, the sinful flesh and blood remains within me so that I am not entirely holy and pure but as the Apostle says in Galatians 5:17, 'The flesh lusteth

Luther reintroduced an old biblical principle into theology when he insisted upon justification by faith. Furthermore, he insisted that this principle was equally valid in the field of ethics. Here it found a very special expression as "faith active in love." But if "faith active in love" is Luther's ethical principle, it is important to investigate what Luther meant by "love." If faith expresses itself in relation to our fellow men in terms of love, how is this love to be defined? This question is of the greatest significance in view of the recent investigations of the differences that obscure a clear understanding of the word "love" and its uses in Christian theology. Holl and after him Nygren [45] have shown that it was customary for Roman Catholic theologians to speak of love in very general terms and to distinguish between right love and wrong love on the basis of the object being loved. Preparing the way for this interpretation of love, Augustine had said: "All love either ascends or descends."[46] Love that is ethically valuable is the love that ascends; love that is of no ultimate ethical value and may indeed be harmful is the love that descends. Man has to

. . . .

against the spirit, etc.' And he also says of himself in Romans that he must without ceasing fight and war against himself and cannot do the good things he would do. The spirit might want to live pure and perfect according to God's Word, but the flesh is present and attacks and fights so that we look for our honor, greed, good times, and become lazy, bored, and tired of our calling and service. And so there is an eternal struggle and resistance within us. Much that is impure occurs because of this other half of our person. And we are not entirely pure or have a clear conscience and are full of love, even if it may appear so to other people. But in the sight of God much is missing and much deserves punishment, even if everything seems perfect in the sight of man."

[45] Holl, *Gesammelte Aufsätze,* III; Nygren, *Agape and Eros,* II, II.

[46] Augustine, *Ennaratio in Psalmum,* Chap. CXXII, I, as quoted in Nygren, II, II, 265.

choose between these two forms of love, which Augustine called *caritas* and *cupiditas,* charity and cupidity.

Augustine considered cupiditas, or the love which is directed downwards, wrong and senseless, since it neglects the highest good, even God Himself. Only caritas is justified from a moral or even a reasonable point of view.[47] But both, charity and cupidity, are to him "love." Thus, love becomes an emotion which is in itself ethically indifferent, and whose worth depends entirely upon the object to which it is directed. As Nygren asserts: "It can be the highest thing—if it is directed to the highest, to what is really worth loving and desiring, to God; but it can be the lowest—if it is directed to the lowest, to temporal transient things. Love is the elementary motive power in all human action, good and bad alike."[48] Augustine encourages charity, the right kind of love, but mainly because in charity the love energy will

. . . .

[47] Augustine, *Ennaratio in Psalmum,* Chap. XXXI, ii, 5: "Love, but watch what you love. The love of God, the love of the neighbor, is called 'caritas'; the love of the world, the love of this age, is called 'cupiditas.'" Cf. Nygren, p. 277. See also Augustine, Letters CXXX (A.D. 412, To Protea), *Nicene and Post-Nicene Fathers,* I, 460: "It might, indeed, appear wonderful that solitude about prayer should occupy your heart and claim the first place in it, when you are, so far as this world is concerned, noble and wealthy, and the mother of such an illustrious family, and, although a widow, not desolate, *were it not that you wisely understand that in this world and in this life the soul has no sure position."*

[48] Nygren, p. 276. See also Augustine, Sermon XLVI (I John 2:15), *Nicene and Post-Nicene Fathers,* VI, 408: "We know what great things love itself can do. Very often is this love even abominable and impure; but how great hardships have men suffered, what indignities and intolerable things have they endured, to attain to the object of their love? Whether it be a lover of money who is called covetous; or a lover of honour, who is called ambitious; or a lover of beautiful women, who is called voluptuous. And who could enumerate all sorts of loves? . . Since then the majority of men are such as their loves are, and

94

be used in the manner most conducive to the eternal happiness of the individual. "The soul which vainly sought its desired happiness in the world must turn to God and seek in Him the satisfaction of its desire. Betrayed by the world in its quest for riches, honour, and life, it turns back upon this world and seeks satisfaction in another, where these advantages can be gained, but in a still higher form and for perpetuity."[49]

Against this prudential conception of love, which had been developed even further by scholasticism, Luther placed what he considered the "biblical" conception of love. According to Luther, Christian love is diametrically opposed to all human acquisitive desire. Love, insofar as it is truly Christian, is modeled after the love of Christ. It is a love that does not consider self-interest; it is, in fact, the judgment of God over all self-love.

. . . .

that there ought to be no other care for the regulation of our lives than the choice of that which we ought to love." Augustine, On Psalms, IX, Ibid., VIII, 37: "The foot of the soul is well understood to be its love: which when depraved is called coveting or lust; but when upright, love or charity."

[49] Nygren, p. 277. See also Augustine, *City of God,* Everyman's Library, II, 245 (Book XIX, Chap. 10): "Yea, the holy and faithful servants of the true God are in danger of the devil's manifold ambushes. For as long as they live in this frail and evil-ridden world, they must be so; and it is for their good, making them more attentive in the quest of that security where their peace is without end and assured. There shall the creator bestow all the gifts of nature upon them, and give them not only as good things but as eternal benefits, not only to the soul, by reforming it with wisdom, but also to the body, by restoring it in the resurrection. There the virtues shall not have any more conflicts with the vices, but shall rest with the victory of eternal peace, which none shall ever disturb. For it is the final beatitude, having now attained a consummation to all eternity. We are said to be happy here on earth when we have that little peace that goodness can afford us. But compare this happiness with that other, and this shall be held but plain misery."

Luther knew that, following Augustine, Peter Lombard had claimed that the biblical commandment of love meant that first God is to be loved, then our soul, next our neighbor's soul, and lastly our body.[50] Luther was familiar with this doctrine of ordered love, and knew that it included and justified self-love.[51] Nevertheless, he objected emphatically, and openly opposed what had been considered the proper interpretation of Christian love for more than a thousand years, saying, "Saving the judgment of others and with due respect to the Fathers, in my opinion—I speak as a fool—that interpretation does not seem to be sound which is alleged concerning the precept of loving one's neighbor, whereby it is said that in the precept itself is the loving form with which one loves the neighbor, in that it says 'as thyself.' Therefore, they conclude: It is necessary that thou first love thyself and then after the pattern of thy love for thyself, love also thy neighbor."[52] On the contrary, he said, "I believe

. . . .

[50] Augustine, *City,* II, 89 (XV, 12) : "But we love the Creator truly if He be beloved for Himself, and nothing that is not of His essence be loved, for of Him we cannot love anything amiss. For that very love, whereby we love what is to be loved, is itself to be moderately loved in ourselves, as being virtue directing us in honest courses. And therefore I think that the best and briefest definition of virtue is this. It is an order of love." See also, ibid. XIX, 14; XII, 8, and Peter Lombard, as quoted in W.A., 56 517, note 5.

[51] W.A., 56, 516, 32 ff. (Comm. Romans, 1515-16): "In the comment I have said that love (caritas) is love (amor) not to oneself, but to one's neighbor. . . . Thus, to please one's neighbor is not to please oneself. But this statement of Gregory and of ours seems to be contradicted by that famous distinction and order of loving. For, according to the blessed Augustine, even the Master teaches that 'first God is to be loved, then our soul, next our neighbor's soul, and lastly our body.' Thus, ordered love begins with itself. The answer is that just this is one of those things by which we have been carried away from love (caritate) ." Cf. Nygren, p. 493.

96

that by this precept, 'as thyself,' man is not bidden to love himself, but the vicious love is exposed wherewith he loves himself in fact; that is to say, thou art wholly bent upon thyself and turned to love of thyself, from which thou shalt not be made straight, except thou entirely cease to love thyself and, forgetful of thyself, love the neighbor alone. For it is perversity that we wish to be loved by all, and in all to seek our own; but rectitude is as if thou shouldst do to all men that which thou perversely wishest to be done to thyself."[53] Breaking all precedent and destroying a very practical and comfortable interpretation, Luther said: "Thou shalt love thy neighbor as thyself. Not as if thou oughtest to love thyself; for if that had been the meaning, then it would have been commanded. But so far is it from being commanded, that the commandment (of love to one's neighbor) is, on the contrary, based on the prohibition (of self-love). So thou dost ill in loving thyself. From this evil thou art

. . . .

[52] W.A., 56, 517, 17 ff.

[53] W.A., 56, 518, 4 ff (Comm. Romans 15:2, 1515-16). Cf. Nygren, p. 494. See also W.A., 2, 580, 24 ff. (Comm. Gal. 5:14, 1519): "This, too, deserves our careful attention, that some of the Fathers gathered from the words of this commandment (You shall love your neighbor as yourself) the opinion that 'ordered love' starts with oneself. They said that self-love defines the standard according to which you ought to love your neighbor. . . . But I understand that this commandment does not command self-love but love of the neighbor. It shows that self-love is already in all of us. For if He had wanted this 'ordered love' He would have said, 'love yourself and your neighbor as yourself.' . . . As far as I can see, this commandment speaks of the perverse love with which everybody, forgetting the neighbor, seeks only his own. This becomes again a right love when man forgets about himself and only wants to serve the neighbor. This is shown also by the members of the body where each serves the other, risking his own safety. For the hand fights for the head and receives injuries in its stead, the feet step into the mud and into the water to save the body. But through this ordered

delivered only when thou lovest thy neighbor in like manner
—that is when thou ceasest to love thyself."[54] It is important
to realize that Luther brought about a complete change in
the generally accepted definition of love. Up to his time,
theologians, guided by the principles of philosophical ethics,
had interpreted love in essentially egocentric and eudaimonistic terms, even if these concepts were used in a sub-
limated sense. Love had been acquisitive love. Now Luther
defined Christian love as self-giving, spontaneous, overflowing as the love of God. This love does not ask after the

. . . .

self-love, which Christ wanted to destroy through this commandment, the most dangerous desire to seek our own is nourished."

[54] W.A., 56, 518, 14 ff. (Comm. Romans, 1515-16). Cf. Nygren,
p. 494. See also W.A., 1, 654, 14 ff. (Against Silvester Prierias,
1518): "And this the words of Christ contain: 'He that loseth
his life for My sake, shall find it.' Accordingly, when Christ says
that we are to love our neighbor as we love ourselves, in my
judgment He is speaking of the perverse and crooked love
wherewith a man seeks nothing but his own; which love is not
made straight unless it ceases to seek what is its own, and seeks
what is its neighbor's. This is the opinion of the blessed Paul,
Phil. 2: 'Not looking each of you to his own things, but to the
things of others.' And I Cor. XIII: 'Love seeketh not its own.'
With these words he manifestly forbids self-love."

[55] Matthew 5:45. See also W.A., 1, 354, 35 (Heidelberg Disputation): "God's love does not find, but creates its lovable
object; man's love is caused by its lovable object. The second
clause is evident and it is agreed by all philosophers and
theologians that the object is the cause of the love. They assume
with Aristotle that every power of the soul is passive and
'matter' and that it acts by receiving—whereby he also testifies
that his philosophy is contrary to theology—inasmuch as in all
things it seeks its own and receives rather than confers good. The
first clause is evident, since God's love living in man loves
sinners, the evil, the foolish, the weak, that it may make them
righteous, good, wise, and strong, and so it rather flows forth
and confers good. For sinners are lovely because they are loved;
they are not loved because they are lovely. So man's love shuns

worthiness of the object, it is not concerned with the love-value of man, but "maketh the sun to rise on the evil and the good, and sendeth rain on the just and the unjust."[55]

It is on the basis of this definition of love, as overflowing, spontaneous love that Luther's ethical principle must be understood.[56] If love is really formed by faith, if it is the active tool of faith, then this love must be more than the prudential desire for the highest good. The love which is Christian faith in action must be part of the divine love given to man by God in order that man may pass it on to his

. . . .

sinners and evil men. But thus Christ: 'I came not to call the righteous but sinners.' And this is the love of the Cross born of the Cross, which betakes itself not where it finds a good to enjoy, but where it may confer good upon the evil and the needy. For it is more blessed to give than to receive, says the Apostle. And so Psalm 41:2: 'Blessed is he that considereth the poor and needy.' Yet since the object of the understanding naturally cannot be that which is nothing, i.e., the poor or needy, but that which is, the true, the good, therefore, it judges according to appearance and accepts the person of men and judges according to the things which appear, etc." Cf. Nygren, p. 507 ff. W.A., 36, 358, 35 (Sermon, Nov. 24, 1532): "This is a knavish love, if I am friend to him only who serves me, can help me, and honors me, and hate him who despises me and does not go along with me. Such love does not come from a heart which is good and pure towards everybody but comes from a heart that only seeks its own and is full of love to itself and not to others. For such a man loves nobody for his own self but figures what is in his interest and what he can get out of it. He is not interested in the neighbor."

[56] W.A.T., 5, 397, 7 (5906): "To love God is to love the neighbor." See also W.A., 36, 360, 11 (Sermon on I Tim. 1:5, 1532): "This, however, must be an overflowing love welling forth from within out of the heart like a fresh streamlet or brook which ever flows on and cannot be stopped or dried up or fail, which says: I love thee, not because thou art good or bad, for I draw my love not from thy goodness as from an alien spring, but from mine own well-spring—namely from the Word which is grafted into my heart."

fellow man.[57] For Luther, the love which is faith active towards the fellow man was a gift of God. He considered man merely the tube or channel through which God's love flows. While even Augustine spoke of "using one's neighbor in order to enjoy God,"[58] Luther spoke of faith and love as "placing man between God and his neighbor," as a medium which receives from above and gives out again below, and which is like "a vessel or tube through which the stream of divine blessings must flow without intermission to other people." And he continued: "See, those are then truly godlike men, who receive from God all that He has in Christ, and in turn show themselves also by their well-doing to be, as it were, the gods of their neighbors."[59] This clearly shows what Luther meant by faith active in love: in faith man receives God's love and passes it on to his neighbor. The Christian as a child of God is used by God to mediate the divine love to other men.

It is to the needy neighbor that God wants man to show

. . . .

[57] Ibid., 360, 17: "Then it goes out lavishly and open to everyone who needs it, and meets both good and bad, friend and foe. Indeed, it is ready for enemies well-nigh most of all, as they have more need that I should pray for them and do all that I can, that they also may become godly and be redeemed from sin and the devil. See, that is a love welling out of the heart, not drawn into it, for he finds in that man nothing from which he might draw it; but because he is a Christian and grasps the Word which in himself is quite pure, the same makes his heart also so pure and full of honest love, that he lets his love flow out unimpeded towards everyone, be the person who or what he may." Cf. Nygren, p. 513.

[58] Ibid., p. 517.

[59] W.A., 10, I, 100, 9 (Kirchenpostille, 1522, Titus 3:4-7).

[60] W.A., 17, II, 99, 18 (Fastenpostille, 1525, Romans 13:8); cf. Nygren, p. 518.

[61] W.A., 10, I, (2), 38, 2 (Adventpostille, 1522, Matthew 21: 1-9). See also Tr. Lenker of this sermon: "You ask, perhaps, what

his love: "It is there God is to be found and loved, there He is to be served and ministered to, whoever wishes to minister to Him and serve Him; so that the commandment of the love of God is brought down in its entirety into the love of the neighbor. . . . For this was the reason why He put off the form of God and took on the form of a servant, that He might draw down our love for Him and fasten it on our neighbor."[60]

According to Luther, all ethics, individual as well as social, must be understood from the key-principle of love. "Faith brings you to Christ and makes Him your own with all that He has; Love gives you to your neighbor with all that you have."[61] Faith and hope are man's attitudes in regard to God, but love is the resulting attitude of man towards his fellow man.[62] But since love has its source not in man himself but in the relationship that God has established with man, it does not depend upon the reaction it elicits from the neighbor.[63] Luther considered love not a

. . . .

are the good works you are to do to your neighbor? Answer: They have no name. As the good works Christ does to you have no name, so your good works are to have no name. Whereby do you know them? Answer: They have no name, so that there may be no distinction made and they be not divided, that you might do some and leave others undone. You shall give yourself up to him altogether, with all you have. . . . Thus it is not your good work that you give alms or that you pray, but that you offer yourself to your neighbor and serve him, wherever he needs you and every way you can, be it with alms, prayer, work, fasting, counsel, comfort, instruction, admonition, punishment, apologizing, clothing, food, and lastly with suffering and dying for him."

[62] W.A., 17, II, 278, 11 (Festpostille, 1527, Luke 12:35-40): "These are the most important three parts of the Christian life: faith, hope, and love. The first two look to God and belong above, the third looks to the neighbor and belongs down here. But our papists and work-righteous men have reversed it, go with their works before God and trade with Him, but with their faith they remain below with mankind."

means to an end but the ethical end itself.[64]

Luther saw the social-ethical implications of this principle very clearly. Heretofore that had been called a good work which allegedly contributed to the eternal welfare of the person doing the work. Now Luther insisted that man did not have to do anything for God or some departed saint in order to achieve his own salvation. "Christ has done and accomplished everything for you, atoned for your sins, secured grace and life and salvation. Be content with this, only think how He can become more and more your own and strengthen your faith."[65] The good was no longer evaluated by what it did "subjectively" for the doer but rather it was judged by what it could do "objectively" for the neighbor. He said: "A good work is good for the reason that it is useful and benefits and helps the one for whom it is done; why else should it be called good? For there is a difference between good works and great, long, numerous, beautiful works. When you throw a big stone a great distance it is a great work, but whom does it benefit? If you can jump, run, fence well, it is a fine work, but whom does it benefit? Whom does it help, if you wear a costly coat or build a fine house? And to come to our Papists' work, what does it avail if they put silver or gold on the walls, wood

. . . .

[63] W.A., 36, 358, 23 (Sermon, Nov. 24, 1532): "God has commanded me that I should show my love to my neighbor and favor everybody, be he friend or foe. Just as our Heavenly Father does by letting His sun rise and shine over the evil and the good. And He does good unto those who blaspheme Him day and night and who abuse His gifts through disobedience, blasphemy, sin, and shame. Similarly, He lets it rain for the grateful and the ungrateful alike, gives the gifts of the soil, money, property to even the worst knaves on earth. Why does He do it? Because of His pure love, which fills His heart to overflowing and which is outpoured freely to everybody without exception, be he good or bad, worthy or unworthy."

[64] Ibid., 359, 36: "When God commands me to love the neighbor, He excludes nobody, neither friend nor foe, good

and stone in the churches? Who would be made better, if each village had ten bells, as big as those at Erfurt? ... Whom does it benefit, if you are shaved half or wholly, if you wear a gray or a black cap? ... Who is better for it, if every church had more silver, pictures, and jewelry than the churches of Halle and Wittenberg?"[66]

"Whom does it benefit?" was the key question concerning any work. It must benefit your fellow man and society, otherwise the work is worthless. "If you find a work in you by which you benefit God or His saints or yourself and not your neighbor, know that such a work is not good."[67] Good works are socially useful, they are works done within the community and for the community. "A man is to live, speak, act, hear, suffer, and die for the good of his wife and child, the wife for the husband, the children for the parents, the servants for their masters, the masters for their servants, the government for its subjects, the subjects for the government, each one for his fellow man, even for his enemies, so that one is the other's hand, mouth, eye, foot, even heart and mind. This is a truly Christian and good work, which can and shall be done at all times, in all places, toward all people."[68]

And this Christian love must be directed not to those who,

. . . .

nor evil. For even if a man is evil and does evil to you he does not lose the name 'neighbor.' He remains your flesh and blood and belongs in the commandment, 'Love thy neighbor.' . . . For a Christian must not derive his love from the person, as the love of this world does, e.g., a young fellow from a pretty girl, a miser from money and property, a lord or prince from honor and power, etc. This is all a derived or borrowed love, that cleaves outwardly to the good which it sees in a person, and lasts only so long as that same is there and can be enjoyed."

[65] W.A., 10, I, (2) 40, 27 (Adventspostille, 1522).

[66] Ibid., 39, 5.

[67] Ibid., 41, 5.

[68] Ibid., 41, 7. See also Ibid., 40, 14: "I would not have you

reasonably speaking, are the best risks but to those who are in greatest need. Luther said: "Love does not consider its own reward or its own good, but rewards and does good. For that reason it is most active among the poor, the needy, the evildoers, the sinners, the insane, the sick, and the enemies."[69] And in their eagerness to fight for the right and against wrong everywhere, Christians must remain aware of the temptation to be alert and courageous in defending the rights of the powerful but negligent and cowardly when the wrong is done to the poor and despised. People who choose this easy path and take from the poor to give to the rich are "hypocrites within and have only the appearance of defending the truth. For they well know that there is no danger when one helps the rich, the powerful, the learned, and one's own friends, and can in turn enjoy their protection and be honored by them."[70]

Luther pointed out that it is "very easy to fight against the

. . . .

build me a church or tower or cast bells for me. I would not have you construct for me an organ with fourteen stops and ten rows of flute work. Of this I can neither eat nor drink, support neither wife nor child, keep neither house nor land. You may feast my eyes on these and tickle my ears, but what shall I give to my children? Where are the necessaries of life? O madness, madness! The bishops and lords, who should check it, are the first in such folly, and one blind leader leads the other. Such people remind me of young girls playing with dolls and of boys riding on sticks. Indeed, they are nothing but children and players with dolls, and riders of hobbyhorses."

[69] W.A., 17, II, 101, 6 (Fourth Sunday after Epiphany): "God does not say, thou shalt love the rich, the powerful, the learned, the holy. No, the free love and the most perfect commandment does not apply to such special persons, but it knows no consideration of person at all. It is the false, carnal love of the world which looks only to the person and loves only so long as there is profit and hope. When hope and profit are gone, then love disappears also. But this commandment demands free love for everybody, whoever he might be, friend or foe. This love does not consider its own reward or its own good but rewards and does good. For

wrong which is done to popes, kings, princes, bishops, and other big-wigs. Here each wants to be the most pious, where there is no great need. . . . But when something happens to a poor and insignificant man, there the deceitful eye does not find much profit, but cannot help seeing the disfavor of the powerful; therefore he lets the poor man remain unhelped."[71]

The root of the sorry predicament of Christendom seemed to Luther the obsession of his contemporaries with the idea of obtaining salvation for themselves through their own efforts. If they took Christianity seriously, their entire life centered in these unceasing labors to accumulate enough merits through their own efforts, which included the skillful manipulation of the Church and the neighbor for their own ends, to reach heaven, or at least to escape hell and to reduce the stay in purgatory. Thus the Church as well as the neighbor became merely means to a basically selfish end, the salvation

. . . .

that reason it is most active among the poor, the needy, the evildoers, the sinners, the insane, the sick, and the enemies. Confronted by these people this love has the opportunity to suffer, bear burdens, serve, and do good. This keeps love busy, always and everywhere. And note how this commandment makes us equal before God and suspends all differences of calling, person, rank, and work. For since this commandment is given all men everywhere, a king and prince (if he claims to be a human being) must confess that the poorest beggar and the leper are his neighbors and his equals before God. Therefore, he does not only owe him help but according to this commandment he must serve him with everything he has and does."

[70] Phila. Ed., I, 217 (Treatise on Good Works).

[71] Ibid., I, 218.

[72] Luther believed that the planned uncertainty about the future state, even of the believing Christian, which was such an important part of the official Roman theology, instead of encouraging the Christian life actually undermined it. The official Roman theologians had insisted that the Christian hope must be built on merits; otherwise it is mere presumption. "To

of oneself. This made a real concern for the task of the Church or the need of the neighbor impossible.[72] Under certain circumstances a genuine concern for the suffering of the neighbor might be contrary to the selfish interests of the Christian individual. If, for example, all beggars would be enabled to live useful lives without begging, it might conceivably reduce the opportunities of obtaining merits by giving alms to beggars. Luther, placing the emphasis entirely upon the interest of the neighbor, was more concerned with means for abolishing the cause of begging than merely in half-way measures designed to assist beggars temporarily, but to keep them begging. He said that it is at least as useful a service to help a person to avoid becoming a beggar as to give him alms after he has become one.[73]

At the same time, he insisted that all organized begging on the part of the church-sponsored orders who supported

. . . .

hope without merits cannot be called hope but presumption," said Alexander Halesius. See also the book from which this is quoted: Gustaf Ljunggren's *Zur Geschichte der Christlichen Heilsgewissheit,* Uppsala, 1920, p. 208. Similar views were held by Peter Lombard and Hugo St. Victor. (See Karl Heim, *Das Gewissheitsproblem,* Leipzig, 1911, p. 241 ff.) Against such a view, Luther insisted that the inclusion of human merits as grounds for our salvation is a much more blasphemous presumption. W.A., 40, I, 575, 13 (Comm. Gal., 1535): "This I say in order to confute the pernicious doctrine of the sophists and monks who have taught and held that nobody could know for sure whether he is 'in grace,' even if he does good works according to his powers and lives faultlessly. And this opinion was quite generally accepted as a principle and article of faith everywhere in the whole papal realm. And with this godless opinion they oppressed the doctrine of faith, destroyed faith, perturbed the consciences, took Christ out of the Church, obscured and denied all the benefits and gifts of the Holy Spirit, abolished the true worship of God and established in the hearts of men idolatry and contempt and blasphemy of God. For he who doubts the good will of God towards himself and is not sure that he is 'in grace,' he cannot believe that he has the forgiveness of sins, themselves by begging be discontinued.[74] He suggested that the institutions that had harbored these ecclesiastical beggars be turned into shelters for the sick and needy.[75] This was an indication of the very concrete application of his ethical principle. For Luther the neighbor was no longer a means to an end, but a most real and important end in himself. Therefore, even in the dissolution of these monastic institutions which Luther personally despised, he felt that love should prevail. This led to some very specific suggestions concerning the method by which these monasteries and their inmates should be treated. Those monks and nuns who did not want to leave out of their own free choice were to be given Christian consideration. He said: "Since no one is to be forcibly brought to faith and the Gospel, the remaining inmates, who on account of their age, their belly, or their conscience continue in the monas-

. . . .

that God cares for him, and that he can be saved."

[73] W.A., 31, I, 200, 34 (Exp. 82nd Psalm 1530): "For it is the same work and virtue and as good as giving alms, if one helps a person so that he does not need to become a beggar, rather than to give alms and help those that have become beggars."

[74] W.A., 53, 255, 17 (How to Install a Truly Christian Bishop, 1542): "As far as the mendicant houses are concerned, they should be left to die out. For this is not only an unchristian way of doing things but also a scandalous manner of earning a living. Since they are supposed to have nothing of their own they are merely a daily burden to people and make things difficult. But I wish they would not tear apart the great monasteries, which without having the episcopal title are almost like dioceses. They should rather be turned into schools wherever such schools are needed."

[75] W.A.B., IV, 248, Luther to Elector John of Saxony, requesting that the Franciscan monastery at Wittenberg be turned into a shelter for the poor, September 16, 1527: "Since then this monastery, being an ancient princely burial ground . . . could not be used in a more fitting manner than to dedicate it to

teries, should not be ejected or dealt with harshly, but supported for the rest of their days just as before. For the Gospel teaches us to do good even to the unworthy, as our heavenly Father sends rain and sunshine upon good and evil alike. We must remember, too, that these persons drifted into this estate in consequence of the generally prevailing blindness and error, and that they have not learned a trade by which they might support themselves."[76]

. . . .

the service of God and the poor (in whom we serve Christ Himself). I add to the council's my own most humble request that your Highness would give this monastery . . . to our Lord Jesus Christ for a shelter and dwelling for His poor members."

[76] Phila. Ed., IV, 94 (Preface to an Ordinance of a Common Chest, 1523). When a monastery was dissolved the assets were to be used as follows: "First, to support the persons still remaining in them. . . . Second, to provide those who leave with sufficient funds to find a position and to make a fresh start in life even though they brought nothing with them when they entered the monastery. . . . But the third way is the best, namely, to devote all remaining possessions to the common fund of a common chest, out of which gifts and loans might be made, in Christian love, to all the needy in the land, whether nobles or commons."

[77] W.A., 25, 394, 15 (Comm. Isaiah, 1527-30): "For (God) does not need our efforts but our neighbor has need of our deeds. If we now acknowledge that we have received everything from God, we must as a seal of the recognition do the works of the second table (of the Law). This means to obey parents, not to kill, etc. Then even the seemingly least important works are well-pleasing unto God because of the First Commandment." W.A., 23, 363, 9 (Whether to Flee Death, 1527): "That I know for sure, if Christ Himself or His mother were sick right now, everyone would be so devoted that he would gladly be a servant and helper. Everybody would have daring and courage and nobody would flee but people would volunteer help. All this means that we do not hear what Christ Himself has said, what ye have done to the least, that ye have done to me. And when He speaks of the First Commandment, He continues, the other commandment is like unto it, thou shalt love thy neighbor as

108

In all situations, the Christian constrained by a faith active in love was to give himself to his needy neighbor as God had given Himself to man in Christ. The application of Luther's ethical principle made all service of God, if carried out in this world, service of the neighbor. Luther repeatedly emphasized that God does not need our deeds of mercy but our neighbor does.[77]

To Luther it seemed a Roman perversion of the Gospel to

. . . .

thyself. Here you can hear it yourself that the love to the neighbor is as important as the First Commandment, the love of God. And what you do or leave undone for the neighbor is done or left undone for God Himself." W.A., 17, 98, 37 (Fastenpostille, 1525): "Another question arises: How can love for our neighbor be the fulfillment of the Law when we are required to love God supremely, even above our neighbor? I reply: Christ answers the question when He tells us (Matthew 22:39) the second commandment is like unto the first. He makes love to God and love to our neighbor the same love. The reason for this is, first: God having no need for our works and benefactions for Himself, bids us to do for our neighbor what we would do for God. He asks for Himself only our faith and our recognition of Him as God. The object of proclaiming His honor and rendering Him praise and thanks here on earth is that our neighbor may be converted and brought into fellowship with God. Such service is called the love of God, and is performed out of love to God; but it is exercised for the benefit of our neighbor only. The second reason why God makes love to our neighbor an obligation equal to love to Himself is: God has made worldly wisdom foolish, desiring henceforth to be loved amid crosses and afflictions. Paul says, 'Seeing that in the wisdom of God the world through its wisdom knew not God, it was God's pleasure through the foolishness of the preaching to save them that believe.' Therefore, upon the cross He submitted Himself unto death and misery, and imposed the same submission upon all His disciples. They who refused to love Him before when He bestowed upon them food and drink, blessing and honor, must now love Him in hunger and sorrow, in adversity and disgrace. All works of love, then, must be directed to our wretched needy neighbors. In these lowly ones we are to find and love God, in tell Christians to believe that pilgrimages, the purchase of masses, and the endowing of churches is the proper service of God in this world.[78] He said: "God does not care even if you never build Him a church, if you only serve your neighbor." Looking back at the history of the Christian Church, he observed that there had been times when the leaders of the Church used all the earthly possessions of their institution in order to support the poor and needy. Now, he added, things have been reversed and the possessions of the poor were supporting the waste and splendor of the leaders of the Church.[79] But he who ignores his needy neighbor ignores God.[80] If you try to serve God while your heart is at odds with your fellow man your service will be in reality nothing but blasphemy.[81]

Luther's ethical principle, that the Christian life is a life of faith which must express itself in love towards the fellow man, had to be of fundamental importance for the development of his social ethics. For Luther did not believe that

. . . .

them we are to serve and honor Him, and only so can we do it. The commandment to love God is wholly merged in that to love our neighbors." (Tr. Lenker)

[78] W.A., 10, III, 249, 27 (Sixth after Trinity, 1522): "Now look at the kind of life we have led hitherto. We have been going to St. James, to Aachen, to Rome, to Jerusalem, have built churches, paid masses, and withal have forgotten our neighbor; this now is the wrong side up. The Lord, however, here says, Go and take the money with which you were about to build a church and give it to thy neighbor. Look to your neighbor how you may serve him. It is not a matter of moment to God if you never build Him a church, as long as you are of service to your neighbor." (Tr. Lenker)

[79] Phila. Ed., IV, 50 (Treatise on Usury, 1520): "St. Ambrose and Paulinus, in former times, melted the chalice and everything that the churches had, and gave to the poor. Turn the pages and you find how things are now." Cf. W.A., 6, 133 ff.

[80] W.A., 17, 99, 22 (Fastenpostille, 1525): "These facts restrain those slippery, flitting spirits that seek after God only in great and glorious undertakings. . . . But they miss Him by passing

this Christian service which is the result of the Christian faith should only be rendered to individuals; on the contrary, the Christian must serve the "world," the same "world" which is the kingdom of the devil.[82] However, the response from the neighbor, be he an individual or the member of a collectivity, can in no way modify the concept of Christian service.[83] The Christian acts in society because he knows that it is in the living community that God wants to be served. "To love God is not only a matter of correct ideas, as the foolish monks believe, for to love God means to love the neighbor. For God says, 'If you love me, then think and do that which helps your father and mother, your child, wife or husband, your master or mistress.' This is what I want, see whether you are doing this wherever you can. Then you will know whether you love God or hate Him."[84] He also knows that God has said, "If you want to love and serve me, do it through your neighbor, he needs your help, I don't."[85] This is faith active in love.

. . . .

by Him in their earthly neighbor, in whom God would be loved and honored."

[81] W.A., 10, III, 249 (Sixth after Trinity, 1522): "So God would much rather be deprived of His service than of the service you owe your neighbor, and would sooner see you less stringent in your service toward Himself, if you are pious at the expense of serving your neighbor. Summing up, God wishes you to see first to your neighbor's service and interests. . . . So, if I want to be agreeable to God, I must, in the first place, be reconciled to my brother; if not, I cannot be pleasing to Him. For God rejects the service rendered Him, if the service due our neighbor is not performed."

[82] W.A., 25, 222, 44 (Scholia to Isaiah 35:4, 1532-1534): "So it is clear that the world is truly the kingdom of the devil."

[83] W.A., 16, 322, 8 (Sermons on Exodus, 1524-27, 17:3): "For we must serve the world and do good unto it, even if it repays good with evil."

[84] W.A., 52, 461, 15 (Hauspostille, 1544).

[85] Ibid., 462, 12.

111

VI. THE PRACTICAL PRINCIPLE

It has been the object of the preceding investigations to show that Luther's theological method demanded that all social ethics be grounded in the confrontation of man as a creature with God as the Creator. (See Methodological Principle.) Furthermore, it has been asserted that the principle upon which all ethics rests is the fact of the Divine Love, which should be apprehended in faith toward God and love toward the neighbor. (See Ethical Principle.) It now becomes necessary to examine Luther's practical principle of social ethics.

It is at this point that Luther has been criticized most severely. There are many who say that Luther's ethics, though theoretically sound, collapses when confronted with practical life, and that Luther, when dealing with the problems of society, gave up all specifically Christian notions, fashioning his social ethics on the basis of "natural law," quite independent from any idea of Divine Love and grace.[1] Although Luther's champions have refuted these charges,[2]

. . . .

[1] Eugene Erhardt, *La notion du droit naturel chez Luther,* Paris, 1901. Troeltsch, *Social Teachings,* II. Georg Wünsch, *Der Zusammenbruch des Luthertums als Sozialgestaltung,* Tübingen, 1921.

[2] Holl, op.cit., I. Franz Lau, *Ausserliche Ordnung und Weltlich Ding in Luthers Theologie,* Göttingen, 1933. Herman Jordan, *Luthers Staatsauffassung,* Munich, 1917. Rudolph Sohm, *Kirchenrecht,* Leipzig, Vol. I, 1892, Vol. II, 1922. Arnold, *Zur Frage.* See also Hanns Lilje, *Luther Now,* Philadelphia, 1952.

[3] W.A., 31, I, 409, 34 (Exp. Psalm 111:3, 1530): "These divine callings and orders are instituted by God to assure a lasting, orderly, and peaceful life of the world and to maintain law. For this reason he (the psalmist) calls this righteousness God's which lasts and endures for ever. This is what the jurists call natural law. For if God had not established these callings Himself and

questions concerning the practical principle of his social ethics are at the root of most attacks against him, alleging that he abandoned Christianity when the problems of society confronted him.

What is this controversial practical principle of Luther's social ethics? There can be very little doubt that according to Luther social ethics expressed itself in practice within the framework of the "natural orders." Man as a member of society is a part of certain orders or collectivities such as the family, the state, the empirical church, and his calling. Luther asserted that this membership in the natural orders was part of God's design to preserve the world and to contain the creative forces within man which under the influence of sin might lead to disorder and destruction.[3]

He was convinced that sin and the devil had such tremendous power in this world that sinful mankind left to its own devices in dealing with them would be utterly destroyed. God in His mercy had therefore established the natural orders which counteract the wiles of the devil and guide the destructive forces within man into constructive channels, thus making orderly life possible.[4] This civil justice and

. . . .

if He did not preserve them day by day as His own work, not one spark of law would remain for even an instant. Every servant would want to be master, every maid would want to be mistress, the peasant would want to be prince, and the son would want to be above father and mother. In short, life among men would be worse than life among the wild animals, where one eats the other."

[4] W.A., 30, II, 555, 20; Phila. Ed., IV, 159 (A Sermon on Keeping Children in School): "Therefore, as it is the function and the honor of the office of preaching to make sinners saints, and dead men live, and damned men saved, and the devil's children God's children; so it is the function and honor of worldly government to make men out of wild beasts and to prevent men from becoming wild beasts. It keeps a man's body, so that not everyone may slay it; it keeps a man's wife, so that not everyone may seize and defile her; it keeps a man's child,

peace enables Christians to proclaim the Gospel in peace, and in this manner participate in the ultimate destruction of the "prince of this world."[5] Luther's concept of the "natural orders" was part of his belief that God has not only revealed Himself as the Saviour of men in the person of His Son Jesus Christ but that He reveals Himself to all men as Creator and Lord of nature and history. The revelation in Christ does not destroy this general revelation of God's preserving will as it is expressed in the "natural orders."[6]

. . . .

his daughter or son, so that not everyone may carry them away and steal them; it keeps a man's house, so that not everyone may break in and commit outrage there; it keeps a man's fields and cattle and all his goods, so that not everyone may attack and steal and rob and damage them. There is nothing of this among the beasts, and if it were not for worldly government, there would be nothing of it among men, but they would cease to be men and become mere beasts."

[5] W.A., 23, 514, 19 (Exp. Zechariah 1:7-11, 1527): "The lowest realm, that of the sword, serves the Gospel by maintaining peace among men, without which it would be impossible to preach."

[6] W.A.T., 1, 325, 14 (679, 3): "It is not Christ's opinion that He wanted to suspend and destroy the police force, secular authority, and law. On the contrary, each individual must do in his office what he is called to do, without, however, doing violence to his faith and his conscience. In this way he gives to God that which is God's and to the emperor that which is the emperor's." See also W.A., 30, II, 556; Phila. Ed., IV, 159: "It is certain, then, that government is a creation and an ordinance of God, and that for us men in this life it is a necessary office and rank, which we can no more do without than we can do without life itself, since without government this life cannot continue. Therefore it is easy to understand that God has not commanded it and instituted it in order that it may be destroyed, but that He will have it maintained, as is clearly stated in Romans XIII by Paul and in First Peter 3, where it is said that they are to protect the good and punish the bad. Now who will maintain

The difficulty with this general revelation of God in nature and history is, however, that it is a revelation of God which hides God,[7] just as the human response to this revelation, namely religion, is an approach to God that leads away from God.[8] For an understanding of the place of Luther's "natural orders" in his theological thinking it is important to remember that for Luther, as for St. Paul before him, [9] general revelation, though very real, damns rather than saves man.

According to Luther there cannot be any doubt that man

. . . .

it except us men, to whom God has committed it and who verily need it for ourselves? The wild beasts will not maintain it, nor will wood and stone. But who are the men that can maintain it? Assuredly, not only those men who want to rule with the fist, as many now think to do. For if the fist alone is to rule, things will surely come to such a condition as exists among the beasts, and whoever gets the better of another will stick him in the bag. We have before our eyes enough examples of how much good the fist does without wisdom or reason. Therefore Solomon says in Proverbs VIII, that wisdom must rule, not force. . . . All experience proves this, and in all the histories we find that force, without reason or wisdom, has never once accomplished anything."

[7] W.A., 21, 514, 15 (Sermon for Trinity Sunday): "Behold, Paul's purpose in this epistle is to show Christians that these sublime and divine mysteries—that is, God's actual divine essence and His will, administration, and works—are absolutely beyond all human thought, human understanding or wisdom; in short, that they are and ever will be incomprehensible, inscrutable, and altogether hidden to human reason. When reason presumptuously undertakes to solve, to teach and explain these matters, the result is worthless, yea, utter darkness and deception."

[8] W.A., 12, 291, 33 (Exp. I Peter, 1523): "The pagans have committed a far greater sin by their worship of the sun and the moon (which they considered the true worship of God) than by any other sins. Human piety is therefore pure blasphemy and the greatest sin that man commits."

[9] Romans 1:21 ff.

is by nature religious. It is natural that man should call upon a god; this fact is proven by the pagans, all of whom have called upon idols.[10] However, in their idolatry they have missed the true God. According to Luther, the Jews were also given to idolatry, the only difference being that the Jews had the Mosaic law while the pagans have merely the law which was written in their hearts. But essentially there was no difference. Jews and Gentiles are by nature religious, and this natural religion includes even moral behavior. He said: "It is natural to honor God, not to steal, not to commit adultery, not to bear false witness, not to kill."[11]

For Luther natural and reasonable religion also includes the concept of one divine being, who is eternal and has numerous other divine attributes. He considers monotheism a reasonable, logical conclusion of man and his natural

. . . .

[10] W.A., 46, 666, 26 (Exp. John 1-2, 1537): "Thus saith Paul, 'For the invisible things of Him since the creation of the world are clearly seen, being perceived through the things that are made, even His everlasting power and divinity,' and yet though they knew that there is a God, 'they glorified him not as God, neither gave thanks, but became vain in their reasonings and their senseless heart was darkened.' They became blind and worshiped oxen, calves, pigs, storks, and snakes."

[11] W.A., 24, 9, 28 (Sermons on Genesis, 1527).

[12] W.A., 21, 510, 30 (Sommerpostille, Trinity Sunday, Romans 11:33-36): "(Monotheism) is only a very small part of the knowledge which one ought to have of God, if one does not know any more. For even the pagans see that by means of their reason and deduce it from reasonable causes. Even the pagan Aristotle deduces it in his best book from the saying of their wisest poet, Homer, and says that that would not be a good regime where there is more than one Lord. Just as it is not a good home if there is more than one master or one mistress, to rule and to give orders to the servants. Therefore there must be in everything only one Lord and Regent."

[13] W.A., 19, 205, 25 (Exp. Jonah 1:5, 1526): " 'Then the people were afraid, and cried every man unto his god.' Here

religion, and he does not hesitate to quote the "pagan" Aristotle in order to show that anybody can know about the existence of one deity.[12] The belief in the existence of a god is in all human hearts and cannot be extinguished. Luther will grant that there have been at times people who denied the existence of a god, but he considers such a denial an attempt to close one's eyes and ears by force, in order to avoid knowing about the existence of a god.[13] Reason can tell us that God is, and it is almost impossible to deny the existence of a god. Natural religion is therefore not a theological abstraction, but a reality that confronts us every day.

Luther states further that natural religion is the very source of all religion.[14] Just for this reason it is nothing but idolatry. Even if we can derive from our reason that there is a god, even if we can discover that this divine being

. . . .

you can see how true it is what St. Paul says in Romans 1, and how God is known among the heathen. This means that all the world speaks of a deity and natural reason knows that this deity is something very great above all other things. This is proven here where those who were pagans call on God. Had they not known of God or a deity, how could they have called on him and cried to him? Thus, though they do not have the right faith in God, they hold the view that God is a being who can help on the ocean and in all other needs. Such light and reason are in the hearts of all men and cannot be quenched or extinguished. Though there have been at times men like Epicurus and Pliny and others who denied the existence of God with their mouths. But they do violence to themselves and try to extinguish the light in their hearts. They act like men who hold their ears and eyes so that they do not hear or see. But it is useless, their conscience tells them a different story."

[14] W.A., 28, 609, 29 (Sermons on Deuteronomy, 1529, 5:6): "All the world calls that a god in which a man trusts in need and trouble, which comforts him and whereupon he relies, expecting only good and real help. . . . Through reason men have created many idols. The Romans have made up many gods for the sake of their many concerns and because they needed

is powerful, invisible, just, immortal, and good, what we have found is still merely an idol. As a matter of fact, this natural knowledge about the existence of God is the basis for all idolatry, for it does not bring us one step closer to the reality of God as revealed in Jesus Christ. On the contrary, it leads us into our most terrible sin, the sin against the first commandment. Natural religion is the necessary premise for idolatry. Luther said: "Our reason knows that God is. But who and what he is, who actually is God, that reason does not know. And so reason experiences what happened to the Jews when Christ walked on earth . . . then they knew that Christ was among them and walked with the people. But who He was, they did not know. . . . So reason plays blind man's buff with God and makes always mistakes, and misses every time, calling that God which is not God and again not calling Him God who really is God. Reason would not do either if it did not know that God is, or if on the other hand it knew who or what He is. . . . Therefore in trying so hard, reason gives God's name and honor to whatever it considers is God, but never finds Him who is really God, but always the devil or its own vanity which is ruled by the devil."[15] In other words, natural religion means having a god, but he is a god which can never be anything else but an idol for he is always the creature of our own human wishes and desires. Luther said: "This is the reason why the pagans made gods out of their kings and the Jews tried to make Moses a god. Here is the

. . . .

help. One was supposed to help in war, another could do something else, one could make grain grow, another helped in a shipwreck."

[15] W.A., 19, 206, 31 (Exp. Jonah, 1526).

[16] W.A., 28, 613, 22 (Sermons on Deuteronomy, 1529).

[17] W.A., 19, 492 (Sermon on the Sacrament, 1526): "Although He is everywhere, in all creatures, and I could find Him in stone, fire, water, or rope . . . He does not wish me to search for

source of all idolatry. We are unable and unwilling to notice that God and not the creature works and helps, though the creature may be the means which God uses to work and help and give."[16]

Through reason or through law, man can know idols, but he can never know God apart from His revelation in Jesus Christ. Although, according to Luther, God is everywhere, in every creature, in every stone, in fire and water, He does not want to be found anywhere but in the Word; man cannot find Him anywhere else.[17] And Luther said: "To say that God is present is not the same as to say that God is present for you; God is present for you only when you have His Word and when He through the Word ties you to Himself and says: Here thou shalt find Me."[18]

According to Luther, this Word of God judges all religion, and in the light of this Word all human knowledge about a divine being becomes actually utter ignorance. From this vantage point Luther could say: "That is false religion which can be conceived by reason. That is the religion of the pope, Jews, Turks, like the Pharisee with his 'I give tithes,' 'I am not,' etc. He can go no higher. There is no difference between the Jew, the Papist, the Turk. Their rites indeed are diverse, but their heart and thought are the same: as the Carthusian thinks, so also does the Turk, namely, 'If I do thus, God will be merciful to me.' The same passion is in the minds of all men. There is no middle way between the knowledge of Christ and human working. After that, it does

. . . .

Him there—without the Word, and to throw myself into the fire or the water or to hang myself on a rope. He is everywhere, but He does not want you to reach for Him everywhere. But where He has given the Word, there reach for Him. Otherwise you will not grasp Him but you are tempting God and practicing idolatry. Therefore He has given us a certain manner in which one should seek and find Him, namely the Word."

[18] W.A., 23, 151, 13 (On the Words of Christ, 1527).

not matter whether a man is a Papist, Turk or Jew; one faith is the same as the other."[19]

"One faith is the same as the other"—that is Luther's last word about the saving qualities of all natural theology. Man can have some sense of the divine by means of his reason—but if used by man to save himself this sense becomes utter nonsense.[20] It is important to keep this in mind when examining the practical principle of Luther's social ethics, the "natural orders." For any such doctrine is of necessity an integral part of natural theology. If Luther is so skeptical in his evaluation of the theological results of reason, why does he use the "natural orders" at all? The answer to this question

. . . .

[19] W.A., 40, I, 603, 5 (Comm. Gal., 1531).

[20] W.A.T., 6, 56, 18 (6584): "Therefore all religion where man serves God without His Word or command (even though it may have a big name and reputation) is nothing but sheer idolatry. And the more holy and spiritual they seem, the more dangerous and poisonous they are. For they lead people away from faith in Christ and make them put their trust in their own power, works, and righteousness." See also W.A.T., 6, 58, 37 (6587): "On the roots of idolatry, St. Paul shows them when he says, Gal. 4: 'Howbeit at that time, not knowing God (when you did not know what God's will was as far as you are concerned), ye were in bondage to them that by nature are not gods.' You served the dreams and thoughts of your heart; thus, without, indeed against God's word and command, inventing out of your devotion and opinion a god who could be appeased by words and worship. For just because all men have naturally a common knowledge that God exists, idolatry arose in the world, which otherwise would not have occurred."

[21] Phila. Ed., III, 236 (Secular Authority, 1523): "For this reason, God has ordained the two governments: the spiritual, which by the Holy Spirit under Christ makes Christians and pious people, and the secular which restrains the unchristian and wicked so that they must needs keep the peace outwardly, even against their will."

[22] W.A., 46, 734, 21 (Exp. John 1-2, 1537): "And until the

can be found in his belief that every human life is lived in two realms, the secular and the spiritual.[21] It is important to recognize the difference between these two realms and to keep them separate.[22] Luther claimed that Jesus had emphasized the separation of the two realms when He said, "Render therefore unto Caesar the things which are Caesar's; and unto God the things that are God's."[23] Luther himself pointed frequently to the difference in the two realms and reiterated the need for a clear separation.[24] At the same time he emphasized that these two separate realms are ultimately both God's realms.[25]

He considered one of his important contributions to the

. . . .

end of the world the two realms must not be mixed up as it happened in the age of the Old Testament among the Jewish people. They must be kept separate and apart if one wants to maintain the true Gospel and faith."

[23] Matthew 22:21.

[24] E.A., 33, 7 (Sermons on Genesis): "These are the two realms: the secular, which is ruled by the sword and is seen with the eyes, and the spiritual, ruled by grace and forgiveness of sins. This latter is not seen with physical eyes but only with the eyes of faith." W.A., 51, 11, 21 (Sermon on Psalm 8, 1545): "These two realms are both down here upon earth among the people. For Christ's realm is also here on earth. But there is a great difference, for although both are on earth, Christ's realm and the secular realm, they are ruled and administered differently. . . . The outward and secular realm consists of deeds and force, it needs eyes and fists. But the realm of Christ consists of hearing and faith. I must hear the Word and believe in it, even though this Word may be taught and preached out of the mouths of babes and sucklings. If I believe it I have everything."

[25] W.A., 37, 443, 19 (Sermon on Psalm 65, 1534): "The establishment on earth of secular rule, empires, kingdoms, principalities, cities, councils, and communities and their orderly administration are not the deeds and accomplishments of men but the governance of God." Smith, Jacobs, *Correspondence*, II, 518 (Luther to John Frederic, Duke of Saxony, 1530): "Here we

ideology of his time that he separated the two realms of existence and yet emphasized the divine origin of both.[26] In his explanation of the eighty-second psalm, he wrote: "The secular realm has too long been subjected to the clerical giant and tyrant . . . the reason was that nobody seemed to know the task of the secular authority, and in how far it is separated from the authority of the Church." He continued: "Now the Gospel has been revealed and has shown the obvious difference between the secular and the clerical authority, and it teaches us that the secular authority is a divine order, to be obeyed and honored by all."[27] Luther subdivides the divinely instituted secular realm into a multitude of "offices," "callings," and "ranks." The three main groups of orders within the secular realm are the family (or society, "family" being used in a wider sense than at the present time), the government, and the empirical church. Luther said: "Three kinds of callings are ordained by God; in them one can live with God and a clear con-

. . . .

learn that no prince should trust to his own power or wisdom, nor presume upon it nor brag about it. For no realm nor government stands in human strength or wisdom, but it is God alone Who gives, establishes, maintains, governs, protects, preserves, and Who also takes away. It is all held in His hand and depends upon His power as a ship on the sea or even as a cloud under the sky."

[26] Phila. Ed., V, 35 (That Soldiers, Too, Can Be Saved, 1526): "For I might boast here that, since the time of the Apostles, the temporal sword and temporal government have never been so clearly described or so highly praised as by me. This even my enemies must admit. . . ." W.A., 38, 102, 30 (Defense Against Duke George, 1533): "Well, if I have earned any thanks from this condemned and evil world, and if I had never taught or done anything else than that I adorned and illuminated secular rule and authority, this alone should deserve thanks. Because everybody, even my worst enemies, knows that this understanding of secular authority was under the papacy hidden under the bench and trampled on by the feet of the stinking, lousy priests,

science. The first is the family *(Hausstand)*, the second political and secular authority, the third the church or the ministry," and he added, "after the pattern of the three persons of the Trinity."

"First of all," he said, "you must be a part of a family, a father or mother, a child, servant or maid. Secondly, you must live in a city or in the country as a citizen, a subject, or a ruler. For God has created mankind in order to keep them together in friendship and peace, orderly and honorably. Thirdly, you are part of the Church, perhaps a pastor, an assistant, a sexton, or in some other way a servant of the Church, if only you have and hear the Word of God."[28] These orders are ordained by God in order to assure a minimum amount of peace and justice for the world. Without them men would act worse than animals.

Because the natural orders are divinely instituted, we are not to despise them but rather consider our membership in them an honor and decoration from God.[29] We are not

. . . .

monks, and beggars. . . . Since the time of the apostles no doctor or writer, no theologian or lawyer has confirmed, instructed, and comforted secular authority more gloriously and clearly than I was able to do through special divine grace."

[27] W.A., 31, I, 190, 10 (Exp. 82nd Psalm, 1530).

[28] W.A.T., 6, 266, 16 (6913). See also W.A., 31, I, 234, 15 (On Psalm 117, 1530): "Therewith He approves also all skills, callings, and trades that can be found under such secular authority, whatever they may be called; He approves them in so far as they are honest and laudable according to their own local law, be it burgher, peasant, cobbler, tailor, scribe, horseman, master, servant, etc. For without these callings (says Eccl.) a city or country cannot exist. Therefore we ought to know that such callings are not in themselves opposed to God; and we should not give them up, simply because we want to serve God, and crawl into a monastery, or join some other sect. Yes indeed, all callings are instituted by God, to serve Him through the word in Genesis 3, 'Thou shalt eat thy bread in the sweat of thy face.' That word He wants to have kept."

to cast this decoration aside lightly in order to "run into a monastery."[30] Furthermore, the orders are eternal, even though their empirical character may vary. Essentially God deals with men through these orders until the end of the world.[31] And He deals in this manner with all men, for they are all involved in these orders. To those who might claim that God has not called them, Luther answers: "How is it possible that you are not called? You have always been in some state or station; you have always been a husband or wife, or son or daughter, servant or maid. Take even the least regarded calling. Are you a husband and you think you have not enough to do in that calling, to govern your wife, children, servants, and property, so that all may be obedient to God and you do no one any wrong? Indeed, if you had five heads and ten hands, even then you would not be able to take care of everything, so that you would never dare to think of making a pilgrimage or doing any kind of 'holy' work." And Luther continues: "Are you a son or daughter, and do you think you have not enough work with yourself, to continue chaste, pure, and temperate during your youth, obey your parents, and offend no one by word or deed? . . .

. . . .

[29] W.A., 31, I, 409, 1 (Exp. Psalm 111, 1530): "Here our heart should rejoice, if we find ourselves in a calling founded and ordained by God, and we should gladly thank Him for such a divine work, because we hear and are made sure that our calling is a glory and a jewel in the eyes of God. . . . This means that a servant and a maid, a son and a daughter, a husband and a wife, a lord and a subject are in divinely ordained callings. And if they serve in these callings they are in the eyes of God as beautiful as a bride at her wedding."

[30] Ibid., 409, 14: "But the crazy, blind world does not see this and instead despises these callings so shamefully that it must hurt a godly heart. No, says the world, why should I be in such a low secular calling? I want to serve God and be a monk or nun, a priest or hermit. Such impertinence increased until the world was filled with monasteries and convents of all varieties of orders and sects so that it now crawls and swarms with

124

Again, are you a servant or a maid and do you think you would go idle if you were to serve your master or mistress with all faithfulness as your calling requires, and also keep your youth under control?" And the same holds true of the highly respected callings in life. Luther goes on: "Are you a prince, a lord, spiritual or secular? Who has more to do than you, in order that your subjects may do right, peace is preserved, and no one suffer wrong?"[32]

According to Luther, no one is without some commission or calling and everybody has abundant opportunities to work—if he so desires. And he emphasizes that "masses, bequests, rosaries, prayers and indulgences" are no substitute for faithfulness within and through the divine orders. For "God is not a junkman or a child that can be fooled with a penny."[33] If we are faithful in our calling, we "will have so much to do that all time will be too short, all places too cramped, all strength too weak" to do what is our duty.[34]

Of course, Luther realized that some people use their callings sinfully and pervert them in direct opposition to the will of God. He mentioned as such "anti-callings," robbery, usury, prostitution—and, naturally, the papal hierarchy.[35]

. . . .

'spiritual' people everywhere."

[31] W.A., 31, I, 410, 13: "Human law and order is not constant and fixed. It is not universally accepted everywhere. Rather, we say *novus rex, nova lex:* when an empire changes, its laws change too. But God's callings and orders stand and remain through all changes of government and to the end of the world."

[32] W.A., 10, I, 308, 6 ff. (Kirchenpostille, 1522).

[33] Ibid., 309, 5.

[34] Ibid., 309, 17.

[35] Ibid., 317, 21: "I mention as sinful stations in life robbery, usury, public women, and as they are at present, the pope, cardinals, bishops, priests, monks, and nuns, who neither preach nor listen to preaching. For these callings are surely against God, where they only say mass and sing and are not busy with God's Word, so that an ordinary woman may much sooner enter

But with the exception of those few callings which he considers clearly sinful, he finds all callings good and well-pleasing to God. And he insists on the clear distinction between the value and honor of the calling and its opportunities for Christian service, and the perverse and evil use of an essentially good calling. He said: "A distinction must be made between an occupation and the man who is in it, between a work and the doer of it. An occupation or a work can be good and right in itself and yet be bad and wrong if the man in the occupation, or the doer of the work is not good and right, or does not do his duty rightly. The office of a judge is a precious and godly office, whether it be that of *Mundrichter* or that of *Faustrichter,* whom we call executioner. But when the office is assumed by one to whom it has not been committed or by one who, though it has been committed to him, discharges its duties with a view to securing money or favor, then it is no longer right or good. The married state, also, is precious and godly, but there is many a rascal and knave in it. It is just the same with the

. . . .

heaven than one of these."

[36] Phila. Ed., V, 34 (That Soldiers, Too, Can Be Saved, 1526).

[37] W.A., 15, 625, 6 ff. (Sermons, 1524).

[38] W.A., 15, 368, 18 (Exp. Psalm 127, 1524): "If God does not first put it there man cannot find anything even if the entire world should search and work itself to death. We can see that with our eyes and grasp it with our hands, and yet we don't believe it. Furthermore, where He does not counsel and protect, nothing can be kept even if we placed one hundred thousand padlocks before it. It blows away and disappears so that nobody knows where it can be found. Listen, who put the silver and gold into the mountains so that it can be found there? Who puts the power into the soil so that it brings forth grain and wine and all the fruits to feed the animals? Does man's work do it? Sure, work finds it, but God has to place it there first so that work can find it. Who gives the body the power to propagate the species, so that birds, beasts, and fish are born? Does our work

occupation or work of the soldier; in itself it is right and godly, but we must see to it that the persons who are in the occupation and who do the work are the right kind of persons, godly and upright."[36]

The callings are good and part of God's natural orders, and the practical instruments of Luther's social ethics. God, the Creator, uses them to make us serve each other. It is through our calling that we are forced to do God's will and render services to others which otherwise we might fail to offer because of our selfishness, laziness, and pride.[37] Yet at all times it is God who blesses our work in our calling for our benefit. It is ultimately not our work, but God's blessing which nourishes us, clothes us, and even propagates the race. We do not really create anything, but, using the natural orders and callings, God works through us, creating and preserving everything.[38]

Luther considered marriage an outstanding example of such a divine natural order [39] and termed the devaluation of marriage through the institution of celibacy a "popish

. . . .

and care do that? Of course not; God is present and secretly gives His blessing so that there is plenty. So we must conclude that all our work is nothing else but to discover God's gifts and to store them. We create and preserve nothing."

39] W.A., 40, III, 207, 36 (Comm. Psalm 127, 1532-33): "God, therefore, placed all His saints either into positions of responsibility for family or the state (vel oeconomiam vel politiam), except Christ alone, who was the wisdom of the Father. He neither took a wife nor ruled a secular state, since He had to be something far different from all others. Yet He honored both callings, marriage and governmental authority." W.A.T., 4, 532 (4814): "The estate of matrimony is in importance second only to religion. There are many reasons for its importance, yet most people, like the cattle in the fields and the scum of the earth, flee it because it means personal unhappiness. They are like people who, fleeing the rain, fall into the water. Enter marriage with confidence in the Lord's name and accept your cross. It is important to obey God's order and command for the sake of the heresy."[40] He said that a believing Christian housewife is better than all the nunneries.[41] The estate of marriage is created by the divine word and thus is an order of God well-pleasing to Him.[42] Luther goes so far as to say that "heaven and earth and all creatures were created for the sake of the estate of matrimony,"[43] and that without this estate an ordered society would be quite impossible since

. . . .

propagation of the race. And even if that were not the reason for entering marriage, we ought to remember that it is a medicine against sin and a defense against unchastity."

[40] W.A.T., 4, 263 (4368): "The shameful and dangerous superstition called celibacy and the unmarried life of the clergy under the papacy prevented much that is good. Especially the procreation of children and the strengthening of society and family. At the same time it was also the cause of many scandalous sins and helped to promote them." W.A., 42, 617, 2 (Lectures on Genesis, 1535-45): "The Holy Spirit anticipated the heresy of the papists concerning celibacy, because He teaches that Adam was united with Eve according to God's institution."

[41] W.A., 30, III, 505, 30 (An Example of Papal Doctrine 1531): "Behold what kind of doctrine and opinion Satan has introduced into the church through these people. Now you should realize that among Christians one housewife, even the most humble, if she is faithful, is better than the innumerable convents of all the nuns. And all these taken together are not worthy to put on the shoes of one such housewife because of their blasphemous and sacrilegious orders, or better abominations against God and Christ."

[42] W.A., 49, 799, 6 (Sermon, 1545): "Marriage is an ordinance and establishment of God. When He created man and woman He placed them into this calling so that they could live godly and honestly, pure and chaste. And they should beget children and increase the world and the kingdom of God." W.A., 34, I, 57, 21 (Sermon, 1531): "You speak as a Christian of matrimony if you glory in the fact that God has placed His Word upon it. And His Word is written on each spouse so that you must see them as if they were the only persons and no others on earth and no king in his jewels, or even the very sun itself, should

128

all other estates are derived from it.[44]

The divine character of the natural orders explains also Luther's much publicized attitude towards government or secular authority. This order is also instituted and preserved by God, and is therefore a divine order.[45] Luther emphasizes the emergency character of secular authority as we know it. It is an institution for the days between the times. "Because

. . . .

appear more beautiful in your eyes. For you have the Word by which God has given you this woman or this man and says to you: He is your husband, she is your wife, I am pleased and all angels and creatures rejoice with me."

[43] W.A., 46, 614 (Exp. John 1-2, 1537).

[44] W.A., 52, 395, 39 ff. (Hauspostille, 1544): "Servant and maid, master and mistress, each in his calling has God's word on his side. They can say: 'God has ordered me to do this. In His name I shall rise and go to work, lie down, and sit at the table, etc.' Whatever we do, even if it is merely to sweep the room, it is well-done and done in obedience to God. For the word, 'Honor thy father and mother,' includes all callings, offices, and works which are part of the estate of matrimony and are derived from it." Phila. Ed., III, 423 (To the Knights of the Teutonic Order, 1523): "For this reason also, God has done marriage the honor of putting it into the Fourth Commandment, immediately after the honor due to Him, and commands, 'Thou shalt honor father and mother.' Show me an honor in heaven or on earth, apart from the honor of God, that can equal this honor! Neither the secular nor the spiritual estate has been so highly honored. And if God had given utterance to nothing more than this Fourth Commandment with reference to married life, men ought to have learned quite well from this commandment that in God's sight there is no higher office, estate, condition, and work (next to the Gospel which concerns God Himself) than the estate of marriage."

[45] Phila. Ed., IV, 290 (Exp. 82nd Psalm, 1530): "Now because this is not a matter of human will or devising, but God Himself appoints and preserves all rulership, and if He no longer held it up, it would all fall down, even though all the world held it fast, therefore, it is rightly called a divine thing, a divine

not all men believe, but the majority, in fact, does not believe, God has ordained it that secular authority carry a sword and resist evil so that the world may not devour itself."[46] Luther says that secular authority, if it fulfills its preserving task, is in fact a "mask of God" behind which He Himself works.[47] No secular authority stands or falls as the result of human endeavor or ingenuity; God alone ordains, upholds, protects, or destroys it.

It is from this point of view that one must understand Luther's position in regard to obedience to the natural orders. Such obedience is not obedience to men, but ultimately obedience to God. "It is God who orders you, by means of your parents."[48] And it is God's general procedure in the secular realm, to rule "not somehow from heaven by means of angels, but through ordinary authority."[49] Luther could go so far as to say that by means of the orders God operates through us, so that our words become His words and our actions become His actions.[50]

. . . .

ordinance and such persons are rightly called divine, godlike, or gods. . . . From this we see how high and how glorious God will have rulers held, and that men ought to obey them, as His officers, and be subjected to them with all fear and reverence, as to God Himself."

[46] W.A., 12, 329, 3 (Exp. I Peter, 1523).

[47] W.A., 15, 372, 25 (Exp. Psalm 127 for the Christians in Riga, 1524): "Now you have heard that secular authority must be alert and busy and do everything that belongs to its office. Keep the gates locked, defend the doors and walls, put on armor, store provisions, and act as if there were no God and men had to save and rule themselves. Just as a father must work as if he actually supported himself and his family with his own work. But secular authority must be on guard that it does not rely in its heart on its own achievements and become proud if things go well and worry if it fails. It should let all such preparations and armament be the masks of our Lord God, behind which He Himself works alone and accomplishes what we would like to accomplish. He orders such armaments to hide His work

130

In order to understand fully the divine aspect of the natural orders, we must see them in the light of Luther's general conception of the immanence of God. The God who is present in stone and fire is also present in the orders of nature. But as little as man can find God revealed in any stone or any fire, just as little can man find Him revealed in the natural orders. Apart from the Word of God the natural orders are meaningless; it is through the Word that they become divine orders for us. Luther knows nothing of any immediate, natural laws which receive their validity from some other source besides God, some naturalistic source of values. His secular realm is not at all secular in the modern sense of this word. There is no realm of being which is "autonomous" and not ultimately God's realm. The natural orders are not simply nature with its modern naturalistic connotation. For Luther, nature is always God's nature. And he insists that the natural orders are not even intended to contribute to "the righteousness that makes men good in the

. . . .

behind them and thus frustrates the proud and strengthens the worried, so that He may not be tempted. In this manner He guided all the wars of King David and of the people Israel in the Old Testament. And He still does it today wherever secular authority has faith. In the same manner He made Abraham, Isaac, and Jacob wealthy through their work, etc. So we can truly say that the course of the world and especially the lives of His saints are the masquerade of God, where He keeps Himself hidden and yet wonderfully rules and moves the world."

[48] W.A., 43, 340, 23 (Lectures on Genesis, 1535-45).

[49] Ibid., 106, 17.

[50] Ibid., 70, 5: "This, therefore, is the tremendous glory with which the divine majesty adorns us, that He acts in such manner through us that He says that our word is His word, and our actions are His actions. So that you can actually say that the mouth of the godly teacher is the mouth of God, that the hand which you stretch out to ease the need of the brother is the hand of God."

sight of God. The only thing that can do that is faith in Jesus Christ, granted and given us by the grace of God alone, without any works or merits of our own."[51] An external and civil righteousness is all that obedience to the natural orders and their callings can produce.[52]

The question arises, what are for Luther the immediate standards or norms for the natural orders? All the evidence seems to indicate that he considers natural and positive law the immediate standards. However, he refused to define natural law, for it is for him not a codex of laws, but rather the source of all positive law.[53] To define natural law in some specific codified manner would make it just another positive law and result in confusion. Soon "everybody imagines that he has the natural law in his head."[54] People tend to identify natural law with their own personal predilections. The result is that those "who presume to be in the possession of natural law and who glory in it often become great and glorious natural fools. For the precious jewel called natural law and reason is a rare thing among human beings."[55]

Positive law is the concrete form in which the standards for the natural orders confront man; it is the law pertaining "to certain people, certain persons, certain places, and certain times."[56] In this sense he considers the ceremonial law of the Old Testament the "positive law" of the Jews. As such it was of value at a certain time and in a certain situation, but

. . . .

[51] Phila. Ed., V, 34 (That Soldiers, Too, Can Be Saved).

[52] Ibid., 34 ff.

[53] W.A., 51, 211, 36 (Exp. Psalm 101, 1534-35): "At present one hears much praise of natural law and natural reason, and they say that all written law is derived from them. And this is, indeed, quite true."

[54] Ibid., 212, 1.

[55] Ibid., 212, 22.

[56] W.A., 43, 442, 13 (Lectures on Genesis, 1535-45).

[57] W.A., 30, III, 225, 24 (On Marriage, 1530): "The Law of

the time of its validity passed.[57] Luther calls the ceremonial law the *Sachsenspiegel* of the Jews and says that it does not concern Gentiles. Although there is a basic agreement in the positive law of all nations, this is the result of its roots in natural law. Luther says: "The French do not accept our *Sachsenspiegel* and yet as far as natural law is concerned they agree with us."[58]

In contrast to the Mosaic ceremonial law, the Decalogue is a very good representation of the kernel of the general natural law that goes through all positive law, and as such has unlimited validity. Luther said about this Decalogue, "At no other place has the natural law been put forth in such competent and orderly manner as by Moses."[59] This natural law as found in the Ten Commandments is the basis of all estates and orders in society. It is the norm for all life within the orders of nature, and it is always to be considered as a corrective to the positive law. Suspicious of written law and lawyers, Luther felt that the written law must always be modified and redefined from the unwritten natural law. He thought that justice would be served far better if good judges would rule without being "chained" by the regulations of written law, but he realized also that good judges, through whose influence the natural law would correct the written law, are rare indeed.[60] He therefore considered the written law indispensable for the general use, but in need of constant correction from the norm and basis of natural law.

. . . .

Moses cannot, therefore, be considered completely valid for us throughout. For we must consider the situation and position of our country if we want to institute or exercise justice and law. Our law and our justice are instituted for our country and not for the country and situation of Moses, just as Moses' law was instituted for the position and situation of his people and not ours."

[58] W.A., 18, 81, 12 (Against the "Heavenly" Prophets, 1525).

[59] Ibid., 81, 18.

[60] W.A., 30, II, 557 ff. (On Keeping Children in School).

If one standard of all natural orders is natural law, the other standard is, according to Luther, reason. It may sound strange to hear Luther advocate the use of reason as the criterion for the natural orders, in view of all his criticism of the reliability of human reason. But one must always keep in mind the fact that Luther's criticism of reason is directed at the reason which considers itself a substitute for revelation. In all questions of everyday life, Luther advocates the use of reason for the achievement of reasonable results. He said:

> "This virtue, or wisdom, which can and must guide and moderate the severity of law according to cases, and which judges the same deed to be good or evil according to the difference of heart or intention—this virtue is called in Greek *epieikeia,* in Latin *aequitas;* I call it *Billigkeit* [equity, fairness]. For, because law must be framed simply, in dry, short words, it cannot possibly embrace all the cases and the hindrances. Therefore, the judges and lords must be wise and pious in this matter and mete out reasonable justice, and let the law take its course, or set it aside, accordingly. The head of a household makes a law for his servants, telling them what they are to do on this day or that; there is the law, and the servant who does not keep it, must take his punishment. Now one of them may be sick,

. . . .

[61] Phila. Ed., V, 42 (That Soldiers, Too, Can Be Saved). See also W.A., 11, 272 (On Secular Authority, 1523): "A prince therefore must hold the law as firmly in his hand as the sword and determine with his own reason where law has to be used in all its strictness and where it must be used with moderation, so that at all times reason should rule over the law and thus remain the highest law and the master of all law."

[62] W.A., 43, 106, 26 (Lectures on Genesis, 1535-45): "We, then, with the witness of the scripture, preach civil works. For God

or be otherwise hindered from keeping the law, by no fault of his own; then the law is suspended, and he would be a mad head of a house who would punish a servant for that kind of neglect of duty. In like manner, all laws that regulate men's actions must be subject to justice, their mistress, because of the many, innumerable, various accidents that can happen, and that no one can anticipate or set down."[61]

According to Luther the natural orders are reasonable orders and have to be interpreted by reason. As a matter of fact, politics and economics are the fields where it is not only proper but imperative to use reason.[62] He said quite plainly that in secular matters it is always advisable to follow the judgment of reason.

Of course, if reason is the standard for the natural orders, it cannot be said that these natural orders are immutable. It has been claimed that Luther insisted upon the general and eternal validity of the social system of his time.[63] However, if he admitted the normative character of reason, he had to make allowances for changes of the established orders from this principle. And he did make provisions for such changes.[64]

Luther was not a great friend of change. He felt, from his eschatological outlook (see below), that there was not much chance for a change for the better. This practical conserva-

. . . .

wills that we carry each other's afflictions, and He commands that we should not despair in these afflictions, but be confident that He will be with us. Yes, He even instructs us through natural reason, by which we rule these civil affairs, that we should not tempt God, who has made the earth subject to us."

[63] Boehmer, *Luther in the Light;* Troeltsch, *Social Teachings;* G. Wünsch, *Der Zusammenbruch;* See also Lau, *Aüsserliche,* p. 53.

[64] Lau, op. cit., p. 50 ff.

tism does not imply a principle of static acceptance of all existing orders. Such a principle has been claimed for Luther,[65] but it contradicts his basic attitude in regard to the reformation of the church. His entire appeal to the Christian nobility is an appeal for change—change in the realm of the church, but change nevertheless.[66] Luther believed that history is made and changed by great men and heroes.[67] These heroes, who bring about the changes in history, are the revolutionary antithesis to Luther's basically conservative political thesis. Acting under the influence of special divine guidance, these men are used by God to bring about the necessary changes of the existing political and social conditions. They are the means which God uses to change the concrete expression the natural orders find in any specific historical situation. God, who guides their hearts and gives them courage, also gives success to the work of their hands.

Such heroes can of course be found among the Jewish people, as for example, Samson and David; since, however, they are the corrective to the conservative tendency of the natural orders, they are found among all nations. As examples Luther mentions the Persian king Cyrus, the Greek leader Themistocles, Alexander the Great, Augustus, and Hannibal. These men are not princes and lords by education and background but they are created and driven by God. It is also significant that Luther explicitly states that God may recruit

. . . .

[65] Wünsch, op. cit.

[66] W.A., 6, 446, 27 (Christian Nobility, 1520): "As God Himself repealed His own law when it was used falsely (which He had given from heaven), so He still repeals daily what He has ordered, and destroys what He has created because of the same false use to which it is put."

[67] To the following, see Luther's Exp. of Psalm 101, 1534-35 (W.A., 51, 200 ff.).

[68] Ibid., 207, 19: "Not only does He give such persons at times

136

these special heroes from any estate of society.[68] Noble birth means nothing, divine guidance means everything. Tools of God's creative and preserving will, they are chosen by Him with little regard to formal education and position.

Luther also realized that these "heroes" are rarely aware of the fact that their success is part of the divine plan behind the historical process, and they will frequently attribute their achievements to their own abilities. This does not alter their usefulness in bringing about God's purposes, but it results generally in the personal destruction of the prideful hero. If they do not place themselves individually under the Word of God, their work may be historically successful but the hero himself will perish as the result of his own pride. Luther points out that this divine inspiration which guides the hero and is at the root of his success cannot be inherited. It does not pass from generation to generation according to the laws of royal succession. On the contrary, God wants to be free to give such "miracle-men" and "jewels" wherever and whenever He sees fit to do so. The ultimate success of the heroes is dependent upon their willingness to acknowledge their dependence upon God. Those who do not recognize divine authority may help to accomplish God's plan and yet be destroyed in doing so, but those who seriously consider God and His Word are the true "miracle-men" of God and "rare venison in heaven."[69]

This means that the natural orders are not to be consid-

. . . .

to His own people but also to the godless and pagans, and not only to the families of princes but also to burghers, peasants, and craftsmen."

[69] Ibid., 217, 25: "Where there is a king or prince or an aristocracy which seriously (and note, I say seriously) cares for God and His Word, you can call them God's miracle-men and rare venison in heaven. For they do that not according to reason and high wisdom, but God has touched their hearts and drives them in this special manner so that they do not resist God like other kings and lords but promote His Word according to the

ered the unalterable "law of God." He changes them through men whom He places outside of the generally accepted standards of conduct. Their ethical standards are exceptional and not examples for popular imitation.[70] However, even the "miracle-men" are not outside the realm of ethics. They are "miracle-men," not "supermen." In spite of their exceptional tasks they are still subject to God's orders, in their case the orders of exception.[71] Luther provided for change in the social order through these exceptional men; he wanted to avoid, however, a tendency to make such changes lightly and in an irresponsible manner. Contemplating God's "miracle-men," he said, "Every individual must examine himself to see how far he can go in imitating somebody else. He who is so weak that walking is difficult for him should not consider it a cause for shame that he cannot run as fast as a strong man. His best choice would be to let somebody lead and guide him. . . . Thus if Doctor Martinus cannot write epistles or preach like St. Paul to the Romans or like St. Augustine, it is all right for him to open the book and take a passage from St. Paul or Augustine and follow their example."[72] In every walk of life God has given us "miracle-

. . . .

example of David, as far as God gives grace and help."

[70] Ibid., 213, 6: "The question arises, should we not learn from them and imitate the good example of these wise and great people? Why else would these examples be shown to us? Isn't it the same as in the spiritual estate where Scripture gives us the example of Christ and His saints? Answer: Yes, but who can follow? Indeed, we should imitate good examples in all callings. Only watch that we turn not into monkeys and imitate like monkeys. For a monkey, too, wants to imitate everything."

[71] W.A., 43, 642, 40 (Comm. Genesis): "Therefore, it is proper to excuse the Fathers. But this does not mean we should follow their example. For we must not bring about the dissolution of the laws and of common morality. But let us remain under the common laws unless we have a special calling or a heroic inspiration. But if some fanatic argues from the example of Jacob,

men." Generally it is better for us to follow rather than try to equal them.

In summary, it can be said that Luther's natural orders were for all practical purposes based on natural law and reason. From these two norms they were constantly redefined. Changes in these orders were possible, but only through the medium of the "miracle-men." The natural orders are natural and reasonable. Luther used them to describe the existing situation. He felt that they help to explain the world and the forces that preserve it in a semblance of order. However, they do not reveal God, they are not even a part of theology proper, and they do not tell us ultimately what is right and wrong in the sight of God; in short, they have no saving value.

If we are to understand Luther's skepticism toward the natural orders, we must examine them in their relation to sin. According to Luther, the norms of the natural orders, as well as the orders themselves, are affected by sin. He was aware of the fact that all callings and positions of power are misused,[73] and yet he wanted people to remain in their callings, to do their duty as fathers, rulers, soldiers, or

. . . .

Jacob married two sisters—therefore the same is permissible for me—I answer: This does not follow, for ordinary persons must be distinguished from heroic persons who have unique motivations and inspirations. For God is the Lord (*oikonomos*) and Ruler over all. If He inspires someone in contravention of the common rule, this does not abolish or suspend the rule. We must remain under the common laws and permit God to make exceptions as He sees fit."

[72] W.A., 51, 213, 19 (Exp. Psalm 101).

[73] W.A., 40, II, 533, 30 (Comm. Psalm 45, 1533): "Show me a king who loves justice! All are driven to the administration of justice by ambition or some other vanity; indeed, frequently they persecute the just and embrace and favor the godless. It follows that the courts of princes can truly be called the seat and throne of the devil, since there are almost as many devils as courtiers."

whatever their position might be. A Christian is always a member of the natural orders although these orders cannot be anything but sinful orders. Luther said: "All worldly order and law is misused against the commandment of God."[74] In writing of the princes in this world he said, "There are few princes who are not considered fools or crooks, and they prove it by their actions."[75] "And there is no kingdom so well constituted, that it has not something tyrannical in it."[76] Luther went so far as to say: "Everything which is high and mighty in this world fights against the Word of God. For the multitude, the great, those who are high and mighty, those who possess reason, wisdom, and wealth, they are all against the commandment of God (Psalm 2)—however, without cause and in vain."[77] These and other passages point out clearly how thoroughly the natural orders are infected by sin. The main reason for this situation is that they are administered by sinful men. As long as the world stands, this fact will have to be kept in mind.

. . . .

[74] W.A., 32, 393, 18 (Sermons on Matthew 5-7, 1530-32): "A Christian can without sin engage in the affairs of the world, but he does this not as a Christian but as a citizen of the world (Weltperson), and yet his heart can remain pure in his adherence to Christianity, as Christ demands it. This the world cannot do, but it rather misuses all worldly order and law, indeed every creature, against the commandment of God."

[75] W.A., 11, 270, 15 (On Secular Authority, 1523).

[76] W.A., 42, 481, 5 (Lectures on Genesis); see also W.A., 42, 523, 31: "For as it was in the beginning, so it is now and will be always and forever, that the princes, not satisfied with their own, strive for that which belongs to others."

[77] W.A., 31, I, 27, 16 (Psalm 119 translated and explained, 1529).

[78] W.A., 42, 346, 32 (Lectures on Genesis): "For although we do not condemn economics and politics, nevertheless, the human heart corrupts these things (which are in themselves good) because it uses them for its own glory, benefit, and tyranny

Besides being poorly administered by sinful men, the natural orders also lend themselves to idolatry. They give men the opportunity to express their pride, vanity, and presumption. Those who administer the natural orders forget too easily the source of all their power, and they claim to be gods themselves.[78] Luther emphasized again and again that it is idolatry to put one's trust in princes and authorities.[79] Men should administer the orders in humility, but since pride invariably creeps in, all orders become idols.

In still another way, sin is involved in the question of the natural orders. In our present state they are orders by reason of sin. There is not one of the natural orders that is not also a remedy against sin. For Luther the authority of the princes was justified by reason of sin. Guided by Romans 13, he defined the task of the government as punishment of evildoers.[80] If men were actually Christians, the need for repressive government with the power of the sword would automatically disappear.[81]

. . . .

against the neighbor and against God."

[79] W.A., 16, 49, 34 (Sermons on Exodus, 1524-27). See also W.A., 51, 254, 10 (Exp. Psalm 101): "Both offices, that of the prince and that of his officials, are divine and just. But those who hold these offices and administer them are commonly of the devil."

[80] W.A., 12, 228, 32 (Exp. I Peter, 1523): "It is the will of God that those who do evil be punished and that those who do well be protected, so that concord might be maintained in the world. . . . He has instituted the secular authority to carry the sword and to keep evil in check, so that the people who do not want to have peace are forced to keep peace."

[81] Ibid., 330, 34: "If we all were Christians and would follow the Gospel, the secular sword and power would not be necessary or useful. For if there were no evildoers there would be no punishment." See also W.A., 42, 79, 8 (Comm. Genesis): "The state is a necessary remedy against our sinful nature. For cupidity must be restrained through the fetters of the laws and punishments, in order that it cannot roam around freely.

141

Luther applies this principle to the order of marriage as well as government. Though in existence before sin entered the world,[82] marriage became eventually a medicine against sexual license.[83] In this sense, all natural orders as given now exist by reason of sin, and to a certain degree also as punishment of sin. All who are involved in the natural orders are also involved in all the difficulties, hard work, and troubles that are connected with them.[84] Even the most important and most outstanding of all natural orders imply for those who administer them a great deal of punishment and trouble.[85] The natural orders as they are operating now are not only administered by sinners and directed against sinners, but they are also punishment for sinners. For Luther, the natural orders are most thoroughly involved in sin.

In addition, the natural orders are involved in sin through their standards, namely nature and reason. Nature is for Luther always fallen nature. The world is always the sinful

. . . .

You could therefore rightly say that the state is the realm of sin. As St. Paul says, 'The power beareth the sword for the punishment of the evil.' (Romans 13:4) If, therefore, men had not done wrong through sin, the state would not have been necessary. . . . Why then were laws, why the state necessary? It is a cautery and a terrible medicine, by which the guilty members are cut off so that the rest might be saved."

[82] W.A., 42, 100, 38 (Comm. Genesis): "Isn't it wonderful that God ordained and instituted marriage in the state of innocence? And this institution and ordination is even more necessary now since our flesh is weakened and corrupted through sin."

[83] W.A., 32, 371, 30 (Sermons on Matthew 5-7, 1530-32): "Therefore God has decreed that everybody should have his lawful wife or her lawful husband, in order that all lust and desire should be directed towards these alone. If you keep this order, He wishes you well and gives you His blessing, for it is pleasing unto Him since it is His ordinance and affair."

[84] W.A., 42, 152, 11 (Comm. Genesis): "But his task is made difficult through a definite punishment. For while it is the duty

142

world. As such it stands always against Christ, is full of sin and the enemy of God.[86] Luther said quite frankly: "The kingdom of this world remains the kingdom of Satan."[87] And again: "God has thrown us into this world and under the rule of the devil."[88] Nature always confronts man as corrupt nature, and natural law is therefore always subject to the perversions of sin.

And what is true of one standard of the natural orders is not less true of the other standard. Reason, like nature, in the concrete human situation is always corrupt reason. This is clearly demonstrated by our inability to achieve any reliable knowledge of God by reason alone. It means that although the natural orders are reasonable orders, reason cannot give us a knowledge of that which makes the natural orders important. For example, Luther can say, "The glory of marriage is not understood by the Gentiles and other profane men."[89] Human reason is not only unable to know God, but also unable to appreciate the works of God.

. . . .

of a man to feed his family, and to rule and to govern and to teach, he cannot fulfill these things without particular difficulty and the greatest labors."

[85] Ibid., 152, 22: "But these most illustrious offices have their own punishment added, so that they cannot be administered without the greatest difficulties, as the examples before our eyes show."

[86] W.A., 11, 267, 24 (On Secular Authority, 1525): "For such tyrants act as is expected of worldly princes. They are worldly princes, but the world is the enemy of God. Therefore they must act in opposition to God and in accordance with the world, in order to remain worldly princes and not to lose their standing."

[87] W.A., 44, 647, 27 (Lectures on Genesis).

[88] W.A., 19, 644, 20 (That Soldiers, Too, Can Be Saved, 1526).

[89] W.A., 42, 178, 34 (Lectures on Genesis). See also Ibid., 177, 32: "The Holy Spirit has a purer mouth and purer eyes than the pope. The Holy Spirit Himself therefore blushes not

Although Luther granted reason the power to administer and correct the natural orders, he knew that because of its connection with sin, this very action is involved in sin. It is sinful reason which is the norm for the natural orders.[90] And ultimately reason can be so distorted by sin that it destroys the orders it is supposed to correct. In this connection, Luther referred to the monastic institutions of the Roman church. Although God created marriage, and although it is a reasonable institution, "reason, the clever whore, lifts her nose into the air and goes into the monastery."[91] Although the natural orders are subject to reason, reason proves to be a very unreliable criterion. Both natural law and reason are completely immersed in sin.

Under these circumstances it becomes quite clear why

. . . .

to mention the act of generation, or the union of husband and wife, though these great saints condemn it as impure and base. Nor does the Holy Spirit mention this marriage union in one place only of the sacred record. The Scriptures are filled with such histories." (Tr. Lenker)

[90] W.A., 32, 463, 11 (Sermons on Matthew 5-7, 1530-32): "This is a splendid example which puts us all to shame; we, who are reasonable people and have the Bible, have not as much wisdom as the birds. And we hear our shame sung every time we hear the singing of the birds. For man has gone crazy and has become stupid, since he has fallen from God's Word and commandment; since that time there has been no creature which has not been wiser than he. A little siskin, which cannot talk or read, is now his teacher and master in so far as the Scriptures are concerned, although man has the help of the whole Bible and of reason."

[91] W.A., 10, II, 295, 16 (On the Married Life, 1522): "See here, when natural reason, the clever whore (which was followed by the pagans who wanted to be extra clever), looks at the married life, she lifts her nose into the air and says, 'Oh, am I supposed to put the baby to sleep, wash diapers, make beds, put up with all those awful odors, stay awake nights, get up when the baby cries, take care of eczema and sickness? Or, am I supposed to take care of my wife, support her, work for her, have cares here and there, work here and there, suffer here and

Luther refused to attribute any saving power to the natural orders. They are so completely involved in sin that they actually tend to hide rather than reveal the saving will of God. However, he considers them the practical realm of social ethics. They alone apply to all men regardless of their relationship to the Cross, for they alone are understandable to the unregenerate man. Since, according to Luther, the Christians constitute only a small minority among the nations of the world, practical norms for society cannot be norms that are meaningful to Christians alone.[92] For this reason, God deals with the Christians through His means of grace, the Word, and the Sacraments, but He deals with men in general through the natural orders as they shape nature and history.[93] Here God's preserving and punishing

. . . .

there, and face all the other troubles and worries of the married life? Am I supposed to be a prisoner of marriage?' Oh, you poor miserable man, you have taken a wife, tsk, tsk, so much trouble and worry! It is better to remain single and to live a quiet life without care. I shall become a priest or a nun and tell my children to do the same."

[92] W.A., 52, 291, 3 (Hauspostille, 1544): "What is sin? Is it to steal, to murder, to commit adultery, and the like? These are indeed sins, but they are not the true chief sins. Many persons are not guilty of these manifest sins; but of that chief sin of which the Holy Spirit reproves the world—no one is free, else the Holy Spirit could not reprove the whole world. This great sin is the unbelief of the world, the refusal to believe in Jesus Christ. Nor does the world know anything of this sin before the Holy Spirit reproves the people of it through His teachings; the world considers only such deeds sinful as are contrary to the second table of the Law. It knows nothing of Christ, and much less is it aware of the sin of not believing in Him. . . . The Holy Spirit, therefore, preaches this truth that all men without exception are sinners and cannot of themselves believe in Christ. This is, of course, strange preaching for the world. The world of itself is perfectly ignorant of the duty of having faith in the man Jesus."

[93] W.A., 25, 141, 25 (Lectures on Isaiah, 1527-29, 1532-34):

power can be seen by all.[94]

In summary, it can be said that the practical principle of Luther's social ethics is his concept of the natural orders. He describes them as being divinely ordained and having their source in the preserving will of God. Thus they help to maintain the world until the day of Jesus Christ. However, they are also of an emergency character. In their present form, the family, secular authority, and all the human callings within society are means of directing the creative energy of man, which as a result of sin could easily destroy him, into constructive channels. Marriage and the family make sexual chastity possible. Though at first ordained by God as a means of service, marriage became as a result of sin also the divine remedy against the disease of lust.[95] Authority is also a divine order which precedes the Fall.[96]

. . . .

"As a theological proposition, this passage deals with power; God claims all power; all kingdoms are established and maintained by God. He says: 'I have commanded my consecrated ones.' This passage serves to confirm Romans 13 against seditionists, showing that it is simply not permitted to resist the powers, unless it is done because of a new order and mandate from God." See also Phila. Ed., I, 265: "Therefore, it would be most profitable for rulers, that they read, or have read to them, from youth on, the histories, both in sacred and in profane books, in which they would find more examples and skill in ruling than in all the books of law. . . . For examples and histories benefit and teach more than the laws and statutes: there actual experience teaches, here untried and uncertain words."

[94] W.A., 50, 384, 2 (Preface to Galeatii Capellae, 1538): "History books are nothing but reports, records, and memorials to God's work and judgment. They tell how He maintains, rules, hinders, advances, punishes, and honors the world and especially mankind, giving the bad and good according to their deserts. And though there are many who neither know nor honor God, they run across these examples and historical records and begin to fear that they will experience the same fate as those who are described in these books. This has more effect on them than any

146

However, in the form of secular government it is God's medicine against anarchy, always used by the devil to increase evil. Though Christ rules His people through His Word. He has given to the secular authority the power of coercion to restrain evildoers.[97] The same principle applies to all other orders, the callings and offices in which men live and work. They are not playthings but means of serving God in this world.[98] Luther said: "Each person has his assigned task. A housewife eats her bread in the sweat of her brow when she nurses her child, cooks, and runs her household— even if she does not work in the vineyard, as long as she does her own work. So it is at court, there is plenty of work, think of it my dear counsellor, you are not at court to guzzle wine, etc. Are you a chancellor, a scribe, a knight? Do what is assigned to you willingly and faithfully and you will have

. . . .

simple oral admonition or attempt to stop them by telling them what is the law and the doctrine."

[95] W.A., 43, 19, 28 (Lectures on Genesis): "If you look at the main cause (for the existence of marriage), you will see that through it God has established a church, and healed the foul disease of the flesh through marriage and thus closed a road to sin, so that it can no longer seduce you. And you will have to confess that for these reasons marriage must be highly recommended."

[96] W.A., 24, 71, 31 (Sermons on Genesis, 1527): "The woman does not hear God's word directly but learns from Adam. This shows that even before the Fall the rule and authority was in the hands of the man."

[97] W.A., 12, 330, 30 (Exp. I Peter, 1523): "There are two authorities in the world, just as there are two kinds of people, namely believers and unbelievers. The Christians are ruled by the Word of God, and do not need secular authority for themselves. But those who are not Christians must have another kind of authority, since they refuse to obey the Word of God."

[98] W.A., 52, 62, 31 (Hauspostille, 1544): "Hence, each one ought to regulate his mode of life according to his condition

your reward."[99] Where God has placed man, there should he serve Him. "If you are a student, mind your studies; if you are a maid, sweep the house; if you are a servant, care for the horses, etc. A monk may live a harder life, wear poorer clothes, but he will never be truly able to say that he serves God in this manner. But they who serve society, the state, and the church can say it."[100] And it is through such service that the power of the devil is restrained.[101]

Of course, all these orders are affected by sin, which makes them burdensome and difficult. This is true of the life within the family.[102] And it is equally true of secular authority and every other order.[103] Because they are divine orders they will always feel the brunt of the devil's attack,[104] yet in one form or another they will remain until the end of the world.

It seems quite clear from the above that Luther's teaching concerning the natural orders does not establish a secular source of ethics for society, but that the natural orders are deeply rooted in God's will for the world. However, so far it would seem as if there were no connection between the

. . . .

and calling; living in all propriety, modesty, honesty, and piety, well knowing that the performance of such external duties cannot injure the Christian faith. In the sight of God it matters not whether thou art a man or a woman, an emperor or a servant, a mayor or a watchman; but this He asks of us, that we be obedient to Him, even unto death, no matter what our calling or position in life may be. The shepherds praised and glorified God and were satisfied. They do not say: Henceforth we must serve God by dwelling in the desert, where we can devote all our time to meditation and devotion, free from the cares of everyday life. No, this would not be serving God, but would be an escape from duty, glorifying flesh and blood. If thou remainest in the position which God has assigned thee, thou canst serve God, the man as a man, the woman as a woman, the ruler as a ruler, the citizen as a citizen; each one fulfilling his duty in the fear of God, thus glorifying Him. If thou art faithful in thy calling, giving thanks unto Christ, then wilt thou serve God aright, even without wearing the habit of a ethical principle of the Christian individual, faith active in love, and the divine natural law that governs the orders of nature. But Luther explains that a point of contact between the secular realm and the spiritual realm exists in the person of the individual Christian. In this point the spiritual realm penetrates the secular, without, however, abolishing it. The Gospel itself cannot be used to rule the world, because it is the Gospel and demands a voluntary response from man. It would cease to be the Gospel if it became a new law. But through the person of the believer, who is related to Christ through the Gospel and who is at the same time a member of the natural orders, the faith active in love penetrates the social order. Of the Christians Luther said: "The citizens of the kingdom of Christ are earthly, transitory, mortal men, live and dwell scattered here and there in the lands of this earth and are nevertheless at the same time citizens of heaven."[105] Only they truly understand the divine character of the natural orders.[106] And it is for the sake of the Christians that God maintains the world so

. . . .

monk and without fastings." (Tr. Loy)

[99] W.A., 32, 72, 26 (Sermons, 1530).

[100] W.A., 43, 30, 37 (Lectures on Genesis).

[101] W.A., 32, 142, 24 ff. (Sermon, 1530).

[102] W.A., 44, 326, 27 (Lectures on Genesis): "Verily, marriage is not such an easy life, but it is full of innumerable cares and burdens, full of sweat and hard work."

[103] W.A., 16, 359, 28 ff. (Sermons on Exodus, 1525).

[104] W.A., 37, 426, 34 (Sermons, 1534): "And this is true of all three realms (Church, State, Family), that each has its own devil."

[105] W.A., 45, 212, 21 (Sermons, 1537).

[106] W.A., 29, 599, 6 (Sermons, 1529): "This word, 'Give unto Caesar the things that are Caesar's, etc.,' godly Christians accept with gladness and gratitude because they are illuminated and instructed in regard to the character of government. . . . This

patiently. "He has indeed created all that the world contains and produces for the sake of pious Christians; He gives and maintains all only for their sake, as long as the world stands, in order that they should richly enjoy these things in this life and have no need."[107] Christians alone maintain both realms through their prayers.[108] Luther asserts: "We as Christians ought to know that the entire temporal rule and order stands and remains as long as it does only because of God's order and commandments and the prayers of the Christians. These are the two pillars which uphold the entire world. When these pillars are gone, everything must collapse, as will be seen on the day of judgment. And it is even now discernible that all kingdoms and governments are weakened and are beginning to topple because these two pillars are about to sink and break. For this is the way the

. . . .

peace (which government establishes) is such a great thing that nobody except the Christians gives it any thought and comprehends it."

[107] W.A., 22, 122, 30 (Kirchenpostille). Tr. Lenker. See also W.A., 29, 604, 16 (Sermons, 1529) and E.A., 5, 282: "That crops grow and there is peace on earth does not happen because of the godless multitude, but for the sake of the godly Christians. It does occur that the godless enjoy actually more peace than the Christians, for God is a rich and mild Lord who gives His goods to all the world, even to the godless, as Jesus says (Matthew 5:45), but it happens for the sake of the godly and grateful, even if the evil and ungrateful enjoy it also."

[108] W.A., 29, 604, 12 (Sermons, 1529) and E.A., 5, 282: "The Christians alone uphold the two kingdoms on earth, God's and the emperor's. And they do it with prayer. If there were no Christians and nobody would pray for these two kingdoms, they could not stand, even for one hour. In short, it is for the sake of the Christians that God spares the whole world."

[109] W.A., 45, 535, 3 (Sermons on John 14-15, 1538).

[110] W.A., 24, 273, 6 (Sermons on Genesis, 1527): "This is the answer to the question, 'How can a Christian bear the sword,

world wants it because it does not tolerate the Word of God (which honors and upholds the world) and persecutes and kills the innocent Christians and does not cease to rage against the very pillars which support it."[109] Yet God desires that the Christian take his full responsibility in the world. He may become a leader in secular affairs and even bear the sword.[110] If he attains political power he will at the same time govern his people and serve God.[111] Through the Christian in the world his faith active in love influences the social structure.[112] This Luther stated in the conclusion of his famous *Treatise on Christian Liberty*. He said: "The good things we have from God should flow from one to the other and be common to all, so that everyone should 'put on' his neighbor, and so conduct himself toward him as if he himself were in the other's place. From Christ they have

. . . .

since he is supposed to love everybody?' The Christian does not need the sword for his own sake and not for the sake of the other Christians either . . . but it is needed for the sake of the evil men. Since they must be stopped and the godly protected, a Christian, if he is called by God and by those who stand in God's stead, may go and kill like the others." W.A., 32, 390, 8 (Sermons on Matthew 5-7, 1530-32) "And this is another question, can a Christian take responsibility in this world and rule and administer the law? Is it possible that the two persons (Christian and *Weltperson*) or two kinds of office could be united in one man? Could one be simultaneously a Christian and a prince, judge, lord, servant, maid—which are simply persons of this world since they belong to secular rule? We say yes! God Himself has ordained and instituted secular government and its ranks. He has confirmed and praised it in His Word. Without it this life could not last, and we are all involved in it, indeed, born into it before we even became Christians."

[111] W.A., 51, 244, 34 (Exp. Psalm 101): "And God's help is especially present when David, i.e., godly, Christian princes rule. They serve God and rule the people at the same time."

[112] W.A., 47, 246, 37 ff. (Sermons on Matthew 18-24, 1537-40).

flowed and are flowing into us: He has so 'put on' us and acted for us as if He had been what we are. From us they flow on to those who have need of them. . . . We conclude, therefore, that a Christian man lives not in himself, but in Christ and his neighbor. Otherwise he is not a Christian. He lives in Christ through faith, in his neighbor through love; by faith he is caught up beyond himself into God, by love he sinks down beneath himself into his neighbor; yet he always remains in God and in His love."[113]

Luther could describe eloquently how under the influence of the Gospel a Christian ruler could make the institutions of secular authority the means of service. He suggested to the Christian ruler that he should imitate the example of Christ in his rule. Far from seeing in government merely a means of repression, he portrayed it as a glorious instrument of Christian service. Of the Christian prince, Luther said: "He must consider his subjects and rightly dispose his heart towards them in this matter. He does this if he applies his whole mind to making himself useful and serviceable to them, and does not think, 'Land and people are mine; I will do as I please,' but thus, 'I belong to land and people; I must do what is profitable and good for them. My concern must not be how I may rule and be haughty, but how they may be protected and defended by a good peace.' And he should picture Christ to himself, and say, 'Behold, Christ the chief ruler came and served me, sought not to have power, profit, and honor from me, but only considered my

. . . .

[113] Phila. Ed., II, 342 ff. (Treatise on Christian Liberty, 1520).

[114] Phila. Ed., III, 264 ff. (On Secular Authority).

[115] W.A., 10, II, 295, 27 (On Marriage, 1522). See also W.A., 10, II, 296: "In the same manner the wife should consider nursing, bathing, and all other care for her baby and all other work in which she helps and obeys her husband as truly golden and precious works. . . . And if a man should wash the diapers or do some other job which is commonly considered unfit for a

152

need, and did all He could that I might have power, profit, and honor from Him and through Him. I will do the same, not seek mine own advantage in my subjects, but their advantage, and thus serve them by my office, protect them, give them audience and support, that they, and not I, may have the benefit and profit by it.' Thus a prince should in his heart empty himself of his power and authority, and interest himself in the need of his subjects, dealing with it as though it were his own need."[114]

Similarly he described the faith active in love as it penetrates the difficulties and problems of married life. "What does the Christian faith have to say when confronted by marriage? It opens its eyes and sees all the humble and despised works that are part of married life and, looking at them spiritually, it becomes aware of the fact that they are all adorned with divine blessing as with gold and precious stones. And faith says, 'Dear Lord, because I know that Thou hast made me a man and a father, I know also that these works please Thee. And I confess that I am not worthy to put the baby to sleep or to wash its diapers, nor to care for it and its mother. How have I obtained such dignity that I may serve Thy creature and Thy holy will? I shall do it gladly, even if the works were far more humble.' "[115]

The Christian in the world lives for the purpose of helping others,[116] and through his very existence protects his fellow man from destruction. "If there were no Christians on this

. . . .

man, and everybody should ridicule him and consider him a sissy and henpecked, if he does these works with the conviction I pointed out above and in Christian faith—my dear friend, who has any reason to ridicule him? God and all angels and creatures smile, not because he washes diapers, but because he does it in faith. And those scoffers who see only the work, but cannot see the faith, ridicule God as the greatest fools on earth. Indeed, these scoffers scoff only at themselves and are the devil's sissies with all their cleverness."

earth," Luther says, "no city or country would enjoy peace; indeed, in one day everything would be destroyed by the devil. That grain still grows on the fields, that people get well after sickness, that they have food, peace, and protection they owe to the Christians. For we are beggars (II Cor. 6), yet are making many rich, we have nothing and yet have everything, etc. And it is true that whatever kings and princes, lords, burghers, and peasants have in this world they do not have because of their blonde hair but for Christ's and His Christians' sake."[117]

This explains Luther's personal attitude towards the social order. When he tried to reform schools and churches, restrain usury, counsel fair trade practices, and organize the rehabilitation of the poor, he merely put into practice what he had preached and tried to bring his Christian insights to bear upon the social order.[118] He did not believe that the Christian Gospel could become directly useful to society. The small number of true Christians made such a development unlikely. In order to transform society, Christ uses the Christian individual who lives a life of faith in this world of unbelief. In the believer the secular and the spiritual realm meet. Through him the ethical principle of Luther's social ethics penetrates the practical principle, and the insights of the Christian faith become relevant to society.

Roman Catholicism has confused the two realms of existence by claiming that the church, i.e., the ecclesiastical institution ruled by the pope, must dominate both realms. In this manner the empirical church organization claimed to be able to supply all practical norms for social ethics. The church of necessity became involved in all the all-too-human

. . . .

[116] W.A., 15, 703, 30 (Kirchenpostille): "On this earth man lives not for the sake of works, in order that they may be profitable to him, for he is not in need of them. . . . God does not desire the Christian to live for himself. Yea, cursed is the life that lives for self. For all that one lives after he is a Christian, he lives for others." (Tr. Lenker)

failings of its leadership. It had to give allegedly divine and eternal sanction to forms of social organization which were adequate for one age but which proved quite inadequate in another. Thus, for example, feudalism became the absolute norm for the organization of the state and patriarchy the absolute norm for the organization of the family.

The sects solved the practical problem of social ethics in two different ways. Some simply relinquished the world to the powers of evil and devoted themselves entirely to the contemplation of God and the enjoyment of their own salvation. Others attempted to enforce the Gospel as the law of the world. This made the Gospel a new law and perverted the essential message of Christianity. Since the interpretation of the Gospel as law varied greatly, even the New Testament used as the immediate source of social-ethical standards proved highly equivocal.

Luther, by emphasizing the theoretical separation of the two realms, avoided the identification of the Gospel with any specific program of social organization. By placing the individual Christian who alone is the proper object of the "good news" into the social order, he supplied the natural orders with a Christian social impetus that could exert constant pressure regardless of the particular form of social organization he might confront. Far from making Christianity irrelevant to the social order, Luther made it possible to make the absolute Christian truth ever available to society, not by means of an hierarchical organization or a legal interpretation of the Gospel, but by means of the Christian saint, i.e., the sinner saved by grace, active in the world as the willing tool of God's preserving and saving purpose.

. . . .

[117] W.A., 45, 532, 11 (Sermons on John 14-15, 1538).

[118] The writings of Luther which show his social concern and his personal efforts in the direction of social reconstruction are so numerous that we can only refer to volume six of the Philadelphia Edition of Luther's works and to his many letters that deal with the problems of social reform and reorganization.

VII. THE LIMITING PRINCIPLE

No study of the principles underlying Luther's social ethics would be realistic if it dealt only with those ideas which according to Luther motivate social action. For an understanding of his thought it is of equal importance to examine that principle which more than anything else restrained Luther from advocating as thorough a reformation of the secular realm as he advocated and carried out in the spiritual realm.

Luther felt frequently that the social order needed reformation. He noted that the statesmen and lawyers were also in need of "a Luther" who would attempt to reform the existing organization of society.[1] He gave up all hope that under the law as practiced in his time justice could triumph. "In this life," he said sadly, "the lawyers catch the mosquitoes and flies, but the big hornets and wasps tear through their laws as through cobwebs."[2] And he complained bitterly that everybody cries for justice and law and the entire world is in an uproar for justice's sake; but the quest for justice merely causes war, murder, and strife, so that it could almost be said that the search for justice becomes the cause of all

. . . .

[1] W.A., 51, 258, 6 (Exp. Psalm 101): "I am not impressed by the wiseacre (Meister Klügling) who knows all about secular law and who knows how to do everything better—though I must concede that it seems to me at times that government and its lawyers could well use a Luther."

[2] W.A.T., 1, 1 (2).

[3] W.A., 5, 100, 35 ff. (Comm. Psalms, 1519-21).

[4] Cf. Phila. Ed., I, 173, ff. (Treatise on Good Works); II, 57 ff. (An Open Letter to the Christian Nobility); III, 201 ff. (An Earnest Exhortation for all Christians Warning Them Against Insurrection and Rebellion); III, 223, ff. (On Secular Authority: To What Extent It Should Be Obeyed); III, 403 ff. (To the

injustice.[3]

Yet in spite of all these expressions of dissatisfaction with the existing social order, he showed a remarkable reluctance to take the lead in any thoroughgoing social reform, and often poured cold water on the enthusiastic political efforts of some of his associates. What was the reason for Luther's disinclination to become a social reformer? He was willing to give advice on any economic or political question when the occasion arose. He would lecture on price control, condemn unfair trading practices, advocate compulsory education and decent salaries for the teachers. He would exhort princes and peasants, soldiers and merchants—yet he refused to develop any comprehensive and all-inclusive plan for social reorganization.[4] Everything was merely his personal Christian witness, an attempt to bring his Christian insights to bear upon the problems of society.

The key to the understanding of Luther's reluctance to press for a complete reformation of society was his firm conviction that it was unbiblical to expect such a change so late in the history of mankind.[5] The social-ethical "quietive" which limits in Luther's thought the social-ethical "motive" of faith active in love, is his expectation of the speedily approaching end of this world. Though he was not fanatical on this point and would expressly state that such

. . . .

Knights of the Teutonic Order); IV, 9 ff. (On Trading and Usury and A Treatise on Usury); IV, 89 ff. (Preface to an Ordinance of a Common Chest); IV, 101 ff. (To the Councilmen of All Cities in Germany that They Establish and Maintain Christian Schools); IV, 133 ff. (A Sermon on Keeping Children in School); IV, 205 ff. (Admonition to Peace: A Reply to the Twelve Articles of the Peasants in Swabia); IV, 247 ff. (Against the Robbing and Murdering Hordes of Peasants); IV, 257 ff. (An Open Letter Concerning the Hard Book Against the Peasants); IV, 285 ff. (Exp. 82nd Psalm); V, 29 ff. (That Soldiers, Too, Can Be Saved); V, 75 ff. (On War Against the Turk).

[5] For an examination of some of the eschatological ideas in Luther's thought, see George F. Hall, "Luther's Eschatology,"

views were not to be considered articles of faith,[6] he personally believed that history could be divided into six parts. The first part covered the time from Adam to Noah; the second, Noah to Abraham; the third, Abraham to Moses; the fourth, Moses to David; the fifth, David to Christ; the sixth began with the coming of Christ and will last until the end of the world.[7] Luther was convinced that mankind had arrived at the very end of this last period. Against the astrologers, who defended a circular view of history and hoped that soon a new golden age would dawn, he asserted that the papal rule of the Roman empire was the final stage of the last period of history.[8]

It was this conviction that history had come to an end and that the second coming of Christ was near at hand which made Luther see in all attempts to reform society merely efforts to repair a social order doomed to collapse very soon. He said: "Since no other rule can be expected in (this final period of) the Roman empire as Daniel indicates (2:40), it is not advisable to change it. But let whoever is able to do so repair and patch it the best he can, while we still live, and punish abuses and put bandages and ointment on its pocks. But if you tear out these pocks unmercifully, nobody will feel the pain and the damage more speedily than the clever barbers who rather tear out the

. . . .

The Augustana Quarterly, XXIII, 1944, 13 ff.

[6] W.A., 42, 649, 7 (Lectures on Genesis): "These divisions are arbitrary, and must therefore not be accepted as articles of faith."

[7] Ibid., 649, 1 ff.

[8] W.A.T., 2, 636, 6 (2756a): "The end of the world is here. It has reached the dregs . . . the prophecies of Scriptures are all fulfilled, the Judgment Day cannot be far. . . . If one compares the time that is left with the time past, it is hardly the breadth of a hand, just a little apple left hanging on the tree. Daniel divided the history of the world into the empires of the Persians, Greeks, and Romans. The pope kept up the Roman empire. He was the

wound than heal it. Well, Germany seems to be ripe, and I fear deserves strong punishment. God be merciful upon us! If anybody can improve things I shall say my poor Pater Noster for him if only I could also add the amen. For I have said it again and again (but who will believe me until they have experienced it) that changing and improving are two different things. One is in man's hands and God's decree, the other in God's hands and the result of grace."[9]

Luther felt that this mending and repairing was important. But those who expect to move shortly from a dilapidated house into a stately new mansion cannot be expected to take their present discomfort too seriously. They will be satisfied to repair the leaking roof superficially and to stuff old clothes into the drafty windows rather than tear down the whole house and build a new one. Thus, he felt that Christians in this world are aware of the shortcomings of the present arrangement of society but they also know that a wonderful new home awaits them in the very near future. They cannot take the repair of their present domicile as seriously as those who consider it their permanent home.

Luther believed in social reform, and he tried to do what he could to help in the reorganization of society—but from his eschatological point of view he was unable to take amendments to the constitution of the social orders as he

. . . .

final straw. Now he is collapsing. There are many signs in the sky, on earth there is much building, planting, and treasure gathering. The arts have reached new peaks. I hope the good Lord will put an end to everything and not regard the astronomers who claim that a new golden age will begin in the year [15] 40." See also: W.A.T., 2, 33, 5 (1297): "The Last Day is before our door. My calendar is used up." W.A.T., 2, 216, 11 (1791): "If we defeat the Turks, then Daniel's prophecy is fulfilled and the Last Day has arrived." W.A.T., 5, 110, 12 ff. (5375x); W.A.T., 5, 184, 4 ff. (5488); W.A.T., 5, 205, 19 ff. (5512); W.A.T., 5, 267, 8 ff. (5590); W.A.T., 5, 373, 6, (5826); W.A.T., 5, 135, 1 (6703a); W.A.T., 6, 253, 38 (6893).

9] W.A., 51, 258, 12 (Exp. Psalm 101).

found it as seriously as some of his more secular-minded adherents. Whatever Luther taught and did was in his own mind an attempt to prepare men for the coming kingdom of God that would consummate history on the day of judgment.[10] It was at this point that Luther parted ways with the revolutionary minds of his age. The knights and peasants who were being crushed in the death throes of a disintegrating feudal society hoped that Luther would become the leader of a revolution which would restore their ancient privileges.[11] Luther was quite willing to help with word and deed in order to improve their lot. In his *Admonition to Peace* he said: "We have no one on earth to thank for this mischievous rebellion, except you princes and lords."[12] And a little later he continued: "If it is still possible to give you advice, my lords, give a little place to the will and wrath of God. A cart load of hay must give way to a drunken man; how much more ought you to leave your raging and your obstinate tyranny and deal reasonably with

. . . .

[10] W.A., 25, 88, 19 (Lectures on Isaiah, 1532-34): "Whatever we teach, order, and declare is done for one purpose only: that the godly should learn to expect the advent of their Saviour on the Judgment Day."

[11] Nothing could be more misleading than the claim that the reformation was the cause of the German peasant war. For an examination of this problem see Günther Franz, *Der Deutsche Bauernkrieg*, Munich, 1933, p. v: "The German peasant war does not stand by itself. It was preceded for two centuries by a long, uninterrupted series of local revolts. The peasant war can only be understood in the context of these 'predecessors,' as the last link in a chain of such revolutionary movements."

[12] Phila. Ed., IV, 220 (An Admonition to Peace, 1525).

[13] Ibid., p. 223.

[14] Ulrich von Hutten, Franz von Sickingen, and a considerable number of the lower nobility in Germany felt strongly that the Gospel (and their rights) had to be established by means of force if need be. As early as January 16, 1521, while Luther had ever

the peasants, as though they were drunk or out of their mind. Do not begin a struggle with them, for you do not know what the end of it will be. Try kindness first, for you do not know what God wills to do, and do not strike a spark that will kindle all Germany and that no one can quench."[13]

When the historical situation, however, demanded a decision and he had to choose between social revolution and the reformation of the Church, Luther's choice was obvious.[14] He was unwilling to sacrifice the reformation of the Church and the preaching of the Gospel for the sake of a social and political revolution whose outcome at best could benefit men only temporarily. As the revolution proceeded without him, he was unable to understand how anybody could have the temerity to use the cloak of the Gospel to cover his revolutionary designs. And the wrath which Luther outpoured so profusely against the revolting peasants was the wrath of a man who felt that here were

. . . .

reason to expect a fate similar to that of John Huss, he wrote to Spalatin: "You see what Hutten wants. I would not fight for the Gospel with force and slaughter. The world is overcome by the Word, the Church is saved, and will hereafter as formerly be restrained without violence by the Word." (Smith, Jacobs, *Correspondence,* I, 442. See also Fritz Walser, *Die Politische Entwicklung Ulrichs von Hutten,* Berlin, 1928). Although Sickingen offered Luther protection and the possibility of a revolution which would have given all political power in Germany to Lutherans (see Luther to Link, July 20, 1520, Smith, Jacobs, op. cit., p. 341), Luther numbered him among the "Rottengeister." These "Rottengeister" he accused sharply of using the Word of God to gain personal advantage and the applause of the rabble. Luther's attitude towards the peasants is characterized by the same fear that the Gospel might be misused as a cloak hiding the quest for personal advantage. He said: "Peasants, burghers, and noblemen all use our teaching merely to scratch wealth together." (W.A., 40, II, 158, 22; Comm. Gal., 1535) Luther insisted that God is the enemy of both tyrants and anarchists, people who gambled with mankind's chance to have the Gospel of Christ freely preached, in order to win temporary material advantage.[15]

Those who criticize Luther's position from the point of view of modern political liberalism or Marxism and attack him as politically reactionary because he chose to be a religious rather than a political leader, accuse him essentially of being Luther rather than Karl Marx. From a completely secular and sensate point of view, Luther's reliance upon the power of God seems nonsensical. But it was this "otherworldly" attitude, this complete reliance on God, which made the Reformation possible. Luther succeeded, while the revolutionary heroes, Muenzer and Sickingen, failed.

It has been shown previously that faith was the source of Luther's social ethics; it can now be added that it was also faith that made it impossible for Luther to take any social reform ultimately seriously. Faith was the "motive" and the "quietive" of his social ethics. It was the driving force behind all his attempts to reorganize society and at the same time the reason why all such attempts were in the background of his theological thinking.

It is unfortunate that most attempts to analyze Luther' thought have completely neglected to stress the importance of his eschatology for an understanding of his seeming

. . . .

and "arousing them against each other He brings about the destruction of both." (Phila. Ed., IV, 243)

[15] Phila. Ed., IV, 237: "Again it is not true when you declare that you teach and live according to the Gospel. There is not one of the articles (The Twelve Articles of the Peasants of Swabia) which teaches a single point of the Gospel, but everything i directed to one purpose: that your bodies and your propertie may be free. In a word, they all deal with worldly and tempora matters." See also W.A., 28, 517, 28 (Sermons on Deuteronomy 1529): "The peasants said in their revolt, we too want to wea fancy collars and golden chains, and eat partridges."

political and social conservatism.[16] It must also be granted that Luther's unrealized expectations of an immediate end of the world resulted in an unnecessarily superficial repair of the social structure of this world. It does make a difference whether one is going to inhabit a house for another month or another year. Though Luther was justified in not expecting any ultimate solution of the political and social problems that face mankind, a more thorough repair of the mechanisms that govern men would have made the position of the Church of the Reformation a great deal stronger during the great political and social upheavals that confronted her.

The emergency nature of the reorganization of society, which for Luther included the empirical church, made the princes "emergency-bishops" and proved a serious handicap to a sound development of the Lutheran Church. In 1542 Luther stated: "Our secular lords must now be emergency-bishops *(Not-Bischove)* and protect and assist us pastors and preachers (since the pope and his gang do nothing for us, but rather hinder us) so that we can preach and serve churches and schools. As Isaiah says, '*Reges nutricij tui,*' kings shall nourish you and queens shall nurse you. As it was done in times past almost too generously, and as it is still done where the Gospel has made the godly."[17] Luther never bothered to find a more permanent substitute for

. . . .

[16] See, however, Einar Billing, *Luthers lära om Staten,* Uppsala, 1900, p. 98; Gustaf Wingren, *Luthers lära om Kallelsen,* Lund, 1942, pp. 20 ff.

[17] W.A., 53, 255, 5 (Example, How to Consecrate a Christian Bishop, 1542). See also W.A., 53, 255, 26: "My most gracious lords, Duke John Frederic, elector, and Duke Ernst, have assented and promised as temporal rulers and patrons of the episcopal chapter of Naumburg that they will leave the chapter undivided and a separate corporation as heretofore and take nothing from it. They have done this, in fact had to do this, as patrons of the chapter in order to keep the churches of the

163

this emergency solution. The relatively small interest in world missions which plagued Lutheran orthodoxy for centuries to come was another unfortunate result of Luther's foreshortened eschatology.[18]

Luther himself realized the missionary responsibility of the Church.[19] He said: "A Christian does not only have the right and the power to teach the Word of God, but he has an obligation to do so, unless he is willing to forfeit his soul and bring upon himself God's wrath. . . . And when he

. . . .

chapter faithful to the holy Gospel and the known truth, as true emergency-bishops, in case such a chapter should deviate from the true path. And it is the considered opinion of their electoral and princely graces that this should become a true Christian example for other episcopal chapters, in case they desire to follow for their own sake and the salvation and benefit of their subjects." Cf. W.A.B., 8, 394 ff. (3312), March 19, 1539 (Luther to Gabriel Zwilling): "Now our temporal prince must be an emergency-bishop and emergency-official." See also W.A.B., 8, 396 (3313), March 25, 1539 (Luther to the Church-Visitors in Thuringia) and W.A.T., 4, 378, 25 ff. (4561). Since the Diet of Speyer, Lutheranism had drifted more and more towards a concept of church government which turned the administrative leadership over to the prince of the realm and his appointees. Regardless of the original intentions of the reformers, the practical result of Luther's belief that church government could be arranged with emergency measures, since the world would not last much longer, was the administrative domination of the church by the state. This had very unfortunate results in Germany, e.g., Prussian Union and "German Christians."

[18] In the Lutheran churches of Europe, foreign missions had to develop against the vehement opposition of "orthodoxy" and often outside the established church. For example, although Denmark possessed colonies in the East Indies as early as 1620, the leadership of the Danish Lutheran Church ignored the missionary responsibility which this implied for almost one hundred years. When Lutheran pietism pressed for missions, the leaders of the orthodox movement opposed every attempt to awaken missionary zeal within the Lutheran Church. The

is in a place where there are no Christians, he needs no other calling but that he is a Christian and inwardly called and anointed by God Himself. He is obligated to preach and teach the Gospel to the erring heathen or non-Christians out of his duty of brotherly love, even though no man has called him."[20] He also demanded missionaries, saying, "If all the heathen are to praise God they must know Him and believe in Him. . . . In order to believe in Him they must hear His Word. . . . In order that they might hear, preachers

. . . .

orthodox Lutheran faculty of the ill-fated university of Wittenberg spoke of missionaries as "false prophets," and Pastor Neumeister, a clergyman in Hamburg and author of the popular German hymn, "Jesus nimmt die Suender an," concluded an Ascension Day sermon, in which he had demonstrated to his own satisfaction that the so-called missions are not necessary in our time, with the words: "Vor Zeiten hiess es wohl: geht hin in alle Welt: Jetzt aber: bleib allda, wohin dich Gott bestellt." (In times past the message was, go forth into the world—but now, remain wherever God has called you.) Cf. Gustav Warneck, "Protestantische Missionen" in Herzog, *Real-Encyklopaedie für Protestantische Theologie und Kirche,* Leipzig, 1877-88. Luther's eschatology, which had prevented him from developing detailed ideas on the world-wide missionary task of the church, tended to confuse those followers whose slavish admiration for his words was equalled only by an enormous ignorance of his basic Christian concern.

[19] To the following cf. Walter Holsten, "Reformation und Mission," *Archiv für Reformationsgeschichte,* XLIV, 1953, 1. Luther's attitude towards missions has been the subject of considerable controversy. Some following Gustav Warneck (History of Protestant Missions, New York, 1901), claimed that basic theological considerations of the reformer prevented a missionary emphasis. Others, and especially Holsten, re-examine and question the entire motivation of the modern missionary movement from the theological point of view of evangelical Christianity.

[20] W.A., 11, 412, 11 (Power of a Christian Congregation, etc., 1523).

must be sent to them to proclaim God's Word."[21] And in relationship to the non-Christian religions which he knew, those of the Jews and the Mohammedans, he expressed considerable missionary concern. However, as in the case of the emergency-bishops, Luther seemed to think also of emergency-missionaries. The military prisoners of the Turks had in his opinion a very real responsibility for the conversion of their captors. From his eschatological point of view a thoroughgoing investigation of the missionary problems and methods was as unlikely as had been a basic solution to the church-state problem.

In order to understand Luther's eschatological position, one must remember certain basic tenets of his faith. He considered life an introduction to death and said that from baptism to the grave the life of a Christian is a process of dying.[22] Christians are merely "pilgrims" on this earth; their entire life is a pilgrimage, and they should live as foreigners and guests in a foreign land. It is dangerous to encourage in such visitors and strangers the false notion that the world is actually their fatherland. Luther said: "A pilgrim does not intend to settle in the country through which he passes on his pilgrimage and at the inn where he lodges overnight. His heart and thought are somewhere else. He takes his meals and buys his lodging at the inn, but he keeps moving towards the other place where he is truly

. . . .

[21] W.A., 31, I, 228, 33 (Exp. Psalm 117, 1530).

[22] Phila. Ed., I, 58 (Treatise on Baptism, 1519): "So, then, the life of a Christian, from baptism to the grave, is nothing else than the beginning of a blessed death, for at the Last Day God will make him altogether new."

[23] W.A., 34, II, 113, 19 ff. (Sermons, 1531). See also W.A., 12, 321, 25 (Sermons on I Peter, 1523): "This is the opinion of the Apostle when he says, 'Dear brethren, I beseech you as sojourners and pilgrims.' Since you are one with Christ, as baked into one cake with Him, and His goods are yours and your misfortune His misfortune and He takes upon Himself everything that is yours,

166

at home. Thus Christians are foreigners and guests in this world, but citizens of another country and kingdom, where they have a permanent home."[23]

It was this sort of thinking, derived from his study of the Epistles of Peter, which made it impossible for Luther to attach primary importance to the cares of this world. If the Christian is a pilgrim in this world and if his true interest lies in his homeland, the coming kingdom of God, where he is a citizen, he cannot be ultimately concerned with the affairs of this world. He will participate in the essential activities of men that maintain life and order, even in the foreign land, but he will not become as excited about any of these functions as the person who considers this world his real home. The Christian, according to Luther, will not expect that the problems that ultimately concern him can be solved by means of a reorganization of the social order. This adds a definitely quietistic element to Luther's thinking. The social ethics of Luther has a detached air which prevents him from lightly overestimating the possible accomplishments of social reforms and tends to let him expect the solution of the real problems of the world through the intervention of God rather than the efforts of man.

But what were the reasons for Luther's keen eschatological expectations? It seemed to him that a close examination of contemporary history indicated that the rule of the

. . . .

for this reason you should follow Him. And you should live as if you were no longer citizens of this world. For your goods are not on this earth but in heaven, and if you should loose all temporal goods you still have Christ, who is more than all these things. The devil is a prince of this world and rules it, his citizens are the people of this world. Therefore, since you are not of this world you should act like a guest in a hotel, who does not have his goods there but just takes his meals and pays for them. For this is merely a thoroughfare, where we cannot stay, but we must go on. Therefore we should not use the goods of this world except to clothe and feed ourselves and then be gone to another land. We are citizens of heaven; on earth we are merely pilgrims

Anti-Christ had begun in this world and that the end was at hand.[24] Two factors contributed to this analysis of the situation. One was the power of the papacy, the other the power of the Turks.

The Renaissance popes ruling in Rome seemed to Luther a clear case of the Anti-Christ sitting in the temple of God.[25] The idea that the pope might be the Anti-Christ had dawned on Luther as early as 1519, when he wrote to Spalatin: "I am studying the decrees of the popes for my debate and (I speak in your ear) I know not whether the pope is Anti-Christ himself or his apostle, so terribly is Christ, that is the truth, corrupted and crucified by him in the decretals. I am terribly distressed that the people of Christ should be thus deceived by the semblance of laws and of the Christian name. Sometime I will make you a copy of my notes on the Canon Law, that you too may see what it is to make laws regardless of Scripture simply from ambition

. . . .

and guests."

[24] It is of some significance that Luther's eschatological utterances are not limited to his last years but can be found even in his earlier writings. W.A.T., 2, 31, 32 (1291): "Doctor Martinus was forty-eight years old in 1532 and he said, 'I have one more year to preach, but I am afraid I won't live that long. I hope I shall see the Last Day.'" W.A.T., 2, 216, 7 (1790): "In 1532 Melanchthon said to Luther that the emperor would live to the forty-eighth year. Luther said, 'The world won't last that long, the prophecies of Ezekiel stand against it.'"

[25] W.A., 26, 147, 27 (On Anabaptism, 1528): "Listen what St. Paul says to the Thessalonians: 'The Anti-Christ shall sit in the temple of God.' If the pope is the Anti-Christ, as I most certainly believe, he must not sit and rule in the place of the devil but in the temple of God. No, he will not sit where there are only devils and unbelievers, or where there is no Christ or Christianity, since if he is to be the *Anti*-Christ he must be found among the Christians." W.A., 50, 4, 26 (Preface to Barnes, *Life of the Popes*, 1536): "Slowly, after Christ had been abolished, His apostles and faithful witnesses followed and eventually there

168

and tyranny, not to mention the other works of the Curia, which are like those of Anti-Christ."[26]

What was merely a suspicion in 1519 became a firm conviction soon afterwards, and by 1521 Luther was ready to develop this idea at length.[27] Luther gave many reasons for this view. It seemed to him that the papacy miraculously fulfilled all the biblical prophecies referring to the Anti-Christ, and Luther never tired of pointing out the striking parallels. The pope prohibited marriage in many cases and also demanded abstention from certain foods with the claim that such actions would contribute to an individual's holiness. This seemed to Luther a clear fulfillment of the prophecies of St. Paul about the coming Anti-Christ.[28] Similarly, he pointed out that the Anti-Christ would claim and collect the wealth of the world for himself. This prophecy he saw also fulfilled in the pope.[29] Furthermore, the pope had substituted works and ceremonies for the

. . . .

came a new Christ, namely the Anti-Christ, sitting in the temple of God, with his new saints. He taught us to worship those which neither our fathers nor he himself nor we had known. And this precious new divinity he adorned with indulgences, churches, gold, silver, gems, and all kinds of precious objects. And he distributed the land freely to his worshippers as the Spirit had prophesied in Daniel."

[26] Smith, Jacobs, *Correspondence,* I, 170 (Luther to Spalatin, March 13, 1519).

[27] W.A., 7, 705 ff. (To the Book of Magister Ambrosius Catharinus, etc., with an Exposition of Daniel 8, on the Anti-Christ, 1521).

[28] Cf. Nicolaus Amsdorf's preface to the first volume of the Jena edition of Luther's works. St. Louis Edition, XIV, 480.

[29] W.A., 22, 192, 20 ff. (Crucigers Sommerpostille): "And especially the great rat king at Rome with his Judas purse, which is the great money gulch that in the name of Christ and the church has appropriated to itself all the possessions of the world. For he has reserved unto himself the power to forbid whatever

grace of God, had introduced masses, pilgrimages, and monkish rules,[30] and punished far more severely those who trespassed against his imaginary decrees than those who broke the word, law, and command of God.[31] The pope creates sin where Christ takes it away, calls those who do not worship him "heretics,"[32] and opposes everywhere clearly and consistently the will of Christ.[33] But the clearest sign of all was for Luther the papal claim to be the head of the church. Against this claim he asserted: "The pope is not the head of the church; otherwise the church would be a two-headed monster, since Christ alone is her head, as St. Paul says. The pope indeed is the head of the devil's false church."[34] Summing it up, Luther said: "The Roman Anti-

. . . .

he pleased and again to allow it for money, even to take and give kingdoms, whenever and as often as he pleased, and taxed lords and kings as it suited him. This is a much more infamous and barefaced perversion of the temple of God into a house of merchandise than was perpetrated by the Jews at Jerusalem. For it belonged to Anti-Christ, as is prophesied of him, to levy and collect for himself the treasures of the world; and St. Peter speaking of such a hoard in II Peter 2:3 says: 'And in covetousness shall they with feigned words make merchandise of you: whose sentence now from old lingereth not, and their destruction slumbereth not.'" (Tr. Lenker)

[30] W.A., 40, I, 300, 34 ff. (Comm. Gal., 1535).

[31] W.A.T., 3, 318, 17 (3443).

[32] W.A., 5, 195, 21 (Comm. Psalms, 1519-21): "If you do not want to be burned as a heretic you must worship this Satan and Anti-Christ, who appears under the pretext of the name of Christ, and praise his works as divine."

[33] W.A., 7, 763, 12 (Against Ambrosius Catharinus, 1521): "Since the pope creates sin where Christ abolishes sin, and establishes justice where Christ abolishes justice and chains consciences where Christ liberates consciences, in short, because he does everywhere the opposite, puts sin in the place of grace and the law in the place of faith, how can you still doubt that he is the legitimate Anti-Christ, the abomination standing where it

Christ is a servant of error, an apostle of Satan, the man of sin, and the child of perdition."[35]

This understanding of the position and function of the papacy became an important part of Luther's theology. It was not merely part of his polemic but apart from all personal animosity a sincere theological conviction.[36] Luther claimed that the persecution of the Gospel as carried out by the papacy was not merely the expression of papal ignorance, but the fulfillment of its proper function as Anti-Christ. The pope and his crowd were given to idolatry and servants of the devil,[37] and if the devil himself would rule in Rome he could not do any worse than the pope.[38] The papacy has introduced a perfect system to weaken

. . . .

should not stand?"

[34] W.A.T., 2, 17, 18 (1266). See also W.A.T., 3, 119, 11 ff.; W.A.T., 3, 132, 26 ff. (2985); W.A.T., 3, 562, 18 ff. (3720).

[35] W.A., 5, 653, 10 ff. (Comm. Psalms, 1519-21).

[36] W.A., 12, 392, 14 (Sermons on I Peter, 1523): "You must be armed with Scripture so that you cannot only call the pope the Anti-Christ but also know how to prove it so clearly that you could die with this conviction and stand against the devil in death."

[37] W.A., 52, 177, 3 (Hauspostille, 1544): "The pope and his followers are therefore regular idolaters and servants of the devil. They not only despise the Word, but also persecute it, while they claim to be holy on account of their observances, their hoods and tonsures, their fastings and masses and similar arrangements."

[38] W.A., 54, 268, 31 (Against the Papacy in Rome, Founded by the Devil, 1545): "Indeed, if the devil himself should rule in Rome he could not do worse. If he ruled himself, we could bless ourselves against him (with the sign of the cross) and flee so that he could accomplish nothing. But since the pope has given himself over to him to serve as his mask adorned with God's Word, it is not possible to recognize the devil behind the mask. This is the wrath of God. Then all these things happened which his bitter, devilish, hellish malice against Christ and His church

Christ's kingdom and to promote the kingdom of the devil under the pretext of the name of Christ.[39] Claiming that he can bring all men into heaven, he has actually closed heaven to all men.[40]

Thus, asserting to be the vicar of Christ and closest to God, the pope became the vicar of the devil and farthest removed from God. "Was not this the fate of the pope when he and his followers imagined they were the vice-regents and representatives of and the nearest to God, and persuaded the world to believe it? In that very act they were the vice-regents of Satan and the farthest from God, so that no mortals under the sun ever raged and foamed against God and His Word like they have done. And yet they did not see the horrible deceiver, because they were secure and feared not this keen, sharp, high, and excellent judgment, 'The first shall be last.' "[41] Spreading such errors all over the world and collecting money for them, the pope proved clearly that he is the Anti-Christ.[42]

The powerful position of the papal Anti-Christ revealed

. . . .

could plan. Thus, he with his lies, blasphemy, and idolatry became our idol, which we worshiped under the name of St. Peter and Christ."

[39] W.A., 41, 140, 30 (Sermons, 1535): "But the pope has accomplished most and found the best method to weaken Christ's kingdom and to strengthen and increase the kingdom of the devil (though using the name of Christ and the Church). There is no doubt in my mind that the pope has turned infinitely more souls over to the devil than to Christ."

[40] W.A., 47, 457, 5 (Sermons on Matthew 18-24, 1537-40): "The pope has actually locked heaven for the whole world and at the same time he calls himself the servant of all servants of God, who desires to bring the entire world into heaven. This is good lying, he pretends he would like to see everybody saved and at the same time they are supposed to observe his nonsensical rules."

[41] W.A., 17, II, 140, 21 (Fastenpostille, 1525). (Tr. Lenker)

to Luther that this world was nearing its end. But this conviction was further strengthened by the appearance of the military might of the Turkish empire. The conflict of the Western world with the advancing Turks formed the colorful background of the Reformation. Threatening the empire from the East, the Turks were largely responsible for the inability of Charles V to stamp out the Lutheran Reformation. Since he needed the evangelical princes against this mighty foe, he was in no position to offend them by destroying their religious freedom. For this reason it would have been quite understandable if Luther had looked favorably upon these unwitting allies.[43] But nothing was further from his mind. To Luther the Turks were another indication of the impending end of the world. He saw also in the Turks the power of the Anti-Christ.[44] "The person of the Anti-Christ is at the same time the pope and the Turk. Every person consists of a body and soul. So the spirit of the Anti-Christ is the pope, his flesh is the Turk. The one has infested the Church spiritually, the other

. . . .

[42] W.A., 7, 375, 17 (Cause and Reason for All Articles, etc., 1521): "Let him who wants to do so doubt that the pope, who spreads more than enough of such errors in the world, and who takes land, money, and goods for them from all over, is the true and final Anti-Christ. I thank God that I know him."

[43] Luther was aware of the power-political implications for the Reformation of the threatening armies of the Turks. This is best illustrated by the following episode reported in the *Table-Talk*. A member of an imperial mission to the Turkish Sultan reported to Luther that Suleiman had shown much interest in Luther and his movement and that he had asked the ambassadors Luther's age. When they had told him that Luther was forty-eight years old, he had said, "I wish he were even younger, he would find in me a gracious protector." But hearing that report Luther made the sign of the cross and said, "May God protect me from such a gracious protector." W.A.T., 2, 508, 17, (2537).

[44] W.A., 42, 634, 16 (Lectures on Genesis, 1535-45): "And this interpretation agrees with what Daniel says about Antiochus and

bodily. However, both come from the same lord, even the devil."[45]

Historically, this fact seemed to be verified by their simultaneous origin. He said: "Pope and Turk started out at the same time under Emperor Phokas, about nine hundred years ago."[46] And he advised that the defense against pope and Turk should go hand in hand, since both are expressions of the power of the devil. He counselled Christians to pray against devil, pope, and Turk[47] and often compared the destruction wrought by the pope with the havoc worked by the Turks, explaining that in their efforts to destroy the Church of Christ they complemented each other. "The Turk," he said, "fills heaven with Christians by murdering their bodies, but the pope does what he can to fill hell with Christians through his blasphemous teachings."[48]

. . . .

Paul about the Anti-Christ. He will raise himself over everything that is God and over all worship. For the Anti-Christ, that is the pope and the Turk, does not raise himself above God as far as His divine substance is concerned, which is the unknown and hidden God as Isaiah calls Him. But they place themselves above God as He is preached through the Word and manifest through worship. For both (pope and Turk) do not only neglect the Word and worship of God but hate and persecute them."

[45] W.A.T., 3, 158, 31 (3055a).

[46] W.A.T., 3, 173, 121 ff. (3104b).

[47] W.A., 51, 608, 24 (Call to Prayer Against the Turk, 1541): "Heavenly Father, we have indeed deserved Thy punishment. But execute the punishment Thyself according to Thy grace and not Thy wrath. It is better to be in Thy punishing hands than in the hands of men or enemies. . . . But Thou knowest, Almighty God, Father, that we have not sinned against devil, pope, and Turk and they have no right against us or power over us to punish us. But Thou canst use them as Thy harsh rod against us, who have sinned against Thee and deserved all this misfortune."

[48] W.A., 30, II, 195, 15 ff. (War Sermon Against the Turk, 1529).

Their cooperation indicates the end of the world, for Scripture speaks of two cruel tyrants who will lay waste Christendom when the day of judgment is at hand.[49] And Luther asserted that "no kingdom has ever raged as murderously as the Turk; he is the last and worst expression of the wrath of the devil against Christ."[50] In his "Call to War Against the Turks" of 1529, Luther went into a detailed study of Scripture in order to establish the position of the Turks in regard to eschatology; as a result of his studies he believed that he could say with certainty that the Turk is the same as the Gog, mentioned in Ezekiel 38 and Revelation 20,[51] and a study of Daniel 7 convinced him that the Turks were the "little horn" that would pluck out three of the ten original horns or kingdoms mentioned by the prophet before the day of judgment dawns.[52]

. . . .

[49] W.A., 30, II, 162, 1 ff. (Call to War Against the Turks, 1529): "Scripture prophesies two cruel tyrants who will lay waste and destroy Christendom shortly before the Last Day. One will be spiritual, armed with deceit or false worship and doctrine, opposed to the true Christian faith and gospel. Daniel writes in the eleventh chapter that he will exalt himself above all gods and all worship, etc. St. Paul in his Second Epistle to the Thessalonians, the second chapter, calls him the Anti-Christ. This is the pope and his papacy which we have discussed in other writings. The other horrible tyrant is armed with the physical sword. Of him Daniel prophesies powerfully in the seventh chapter and Christ Himself in Matthew 24; when He speaks of a great tribulation such as has not been from the beginning of the world until now, this is the Turk. Since the end of the world is at hand, the devil must attack Christendom most terribly as a parting shot, before we go to heaven."

[50] Ibid., 162, 19 ff.

[51] Ibid., 171, 15: "There can be no doubt that the Turk is 'Gog' (Rev. 20:8 ff.) who has come from the country Gog or the land of the Tatars in Asia, as the history books prove."

[52] Ibid., 166, 30: "Daniel says that after the ten horns there will appear another horn, a little one among the ten horns. Here

The rule of the pope and the Turk and the general disintegration of society forebodes the end of the world;[53] this was Luther's firm conviction. Since he looked at world history from such an eschatological point of view, he could not expect the solution of the world-historical problems through the normal political activities of the human participants in this drama. On the contrary, only God's intervention could possibly bring about a real solution of the world's problems. This was clearly the time of the Anti-Christ and that meant that history was coming to an end.[54] The Christians, who realized that only God can save man from the power of the Anti-Christ,[55] would have to pray daily for the coming of this Judgment Day. Luther put it: "Oh, that only the day of our salvation and of the Last Judgment would come soon. I desire this day far more avidly than any physical liberation. For in this world we would always get another Mohammed and pope. It would be much better if everything would be overthrown and abolished at once, and with it all the misery and misfortune of this life, than any

. . . .

appears the Turk."

[53] W.A.T., 6, 306, 21 (6984): "When the Turk begins to fail a little the Last Day will surely come. For this is the way it must be according to Scripture. Then the dear Lord will come as Scripture says, 'When I shall come again I shall shake the heavens and the earth and then will come the desire of all Gentiles.' There is commotion enough in the political life at present. Lawyers never had more to do than just now." Cf. Ibid., 34 (6985): "I hope, since the Gospel is despised, that the Last Day is not far off, not more than one hundred years. . . ."

[54] W.A., 45, 46, 14 (Sermons, 1537): "The apostles call this last age the age of Anti-Christ for they saw through the Spirit that nothing of Christ would be left in the Church except His bare name. And also that the Anti-Christ would rule the Church."

[55] Ibid., 47, 19: "For as I have said in this last age, we cannot even hope that this Anti-Christ devil be overthrown and Chris-

mere temporal change."[56] This day alone would bring the final defeat of the powers of the devil. Therefore, "those who are true Christians have no reason to fear this Last Day but every reason to wish for it with all their heart. For as long as they live in this vale of sorrows they will have little peace and rest. Today they are plagued with one, tomorrow with another misfortune. Furthermore, the world is their bitter enemy and persecutes them cruelly. . . . This misery they cannot shed as long as this life lasts. But on the Last Day all this will cease and they will be delivered from all evil. For this reason, Scripture calls this day the day of salvation. And we have no reason to fear but rather should rejoice in the blessed and happy day of the advent and appearance of Jesus Christ our Lord."[57]

Luther claimed that in a sense the day of death is the day of judgment for each individual.[58] This he believed because "in the sight of God there is no counting of time, a thousand years are before Him as if it were one day. Therefore, the first man, Adam, is just as close to Him as the

. . . .

tianity be saved through the Roman emperor or some other great secular power, as it happened in Christendom in times past. On the contrary, the Anti-Christ must himself have the highest power on earth and in addition he must have all kingdoms of the world duty-bound to obey him."

[56] W.A., 44, 613, 20 (Lectures on Genesis, 1535-45).

[57] W.A., 17, I, 220, 35 (Sermons, 1525). See also W.A., 34, II, 474, 32 (Sermons of 1531): "Our daily Lord's Prayer teaches us that we should gladly desire the arrival of the Last Day. And we must cry unto God to revenge His name, blood, and goods on this desperate godless world. No Christian can or should pray differently. . . . Therefore, if you do not desire this day you will never be able to pray the Lord's Prayer or confess the Creed. For how can you say, 'I believe in the resurrection of the body and the life everlasting,' if you do not desire it? If you believe it you must truly wish it with all your heart and love the Last Day." Cf. W.A., 37, 617, 13 ff. (Sermons, 1534).

[58] E.A., 1, 126 (Hauspostille): "Every individual's death is, as

person to be born last, just before the Last Day." He said: "God does not look at time horizontally but vertically. . . . Our reason can see time only horizontally. We must start counting with Adam one year after the other until the Last Day. But before God all these events are in one heap. What is long for us is short for Him. . . . When a man dies, his body is buried and decays, lies in the earth and knows nothing. But when the first man is raised on the Last Day he will think that it hasn't been an hour."[59] At the same time, Luther was convinced that there would be a final day of judgment for the world which would also be a day of joy for the Christians since their suffering would then come to an end. "Therefore, although the signs shall appear fearful and terrible to you, when sun and moon disguise themselves, all creatures are mingled in confusion, and finally the world itself is full of fire, yet you shall not judge by such appearances, but know that this indicates something different, nay, the very opposite to you, from what it does to the ungodly world, which together with its prince, the devil, persecutes you, and does not fear the future judgment."[60] He continued: "As a Christian, you must have such thoughts about the signs of the Last Day, as if you were lying captive among enemies and murderers in a high tower, and your pious ruler should come and begin to besiege the tower with

. . . .

Augustine says, his Last Day."

[59] W.A., 14, 70, 27 (Sermons on II Peter, 1523-24).

[60] W.A., 52, 16, 15 ff. (Hauspostille, 1544). (Tr. Loy) Cf. W.A., 45, 44, 10 (Sermons, 1537): "We Christians all hope for this comforting and joyful advent of the glory of the great God, our Saviour Jesus Christ. (Now He is weak, poor, and despised and in His disciples ever more ridiculed, rejected, spit upon, beaten, crucified, and killed.) We hope that this day is before the gates and will make an end to the innumerable atrocities of the condemned papacy. . . . At this advent Christ will show and prove Himself as our life and hope as we even now believe and preach."

great power, so that everything should begin to fall around you; you would not be afraid of the noise and cannonading, but would much more rejoice, if you knew that it was for your redemption. Thus you should do here too, says Christ."[61]

The Christian must try to remain ever ready for this Last Day. His entire life must be lived in the direction of this day. "Therefore, examine your life, probe your heart to ascertain how it is disposed toward this day. Do not put your trust in your own good life, for that would soon be put to shame; but think of and strengthen your faith in order that the day may not be a terror to you as to the damned, but be your joy as the day of your salvation and of the kingdom of God in you."[62] To forget this day, or to refuse to pray for it would be nothing else but to reject the kingdom of God. To Luther, not to desire the day of judgment is the same as not to desire the kingdom of God.[63]

And here the seeming lack of success of the Gospel and the difficulties that confronted the Church at every turn became for Luther signs of encouragement and assurance that the end could not be far off. With great emotion he said to some of his friends, "God be praised, who has taught us to sigh for the day of judgment and to desire it. While still under the papacy, all the world feared that day, as their

. . . .

[61] W.A., 52, 20, 9 ff. (Hauspostille, 1544). (Tr. Loy)

[62] W.A., 10, I, (2), 114, 28. (Tr. Lenker) Cf. W.A., 14, 71, 31 (Sermons on II Peter, 1523-24): "You know that everything must pass away, both heaven and earth. Consider how you will have to be ready with a holy and godly life as you are approaching this day. Therefore, Peter describes this day as one that is coming even now so that they be ready, hope for it with joy, and hurry to meet it as the day that saves from sin, death, and hell."

[63] W.A., 10, I, (2), 113, 6 (Adventpostille, 1522): "From all this we learn how few there are who pray the Lord's Prayer acceptably, even though it is prayed unceasingly in all the world. There are few who would not rather that the Last Day would

179

hymns, like "Dies illa, dies irae, etc.," indicated. I hope that this day is not far off and we may still see it." Here he was interrupted by one of his listeners who mentioned that when this day approaches the Gospel shall nowhere be preached, since Christ had said that on that day He would not find faith on earth. Luther answered: "What does it mean that we have the Gospel in some corners? Keep in mind that Asia and Africa do not have the Gospel and even in Europe the Gospel is not preached among the Greeks or in Italy, Hungary, Spain, France, England, and Poland. That little speck, Saxony, will not prevent the coming of the day of judgment."[64] Thus the very predicament of man became for Luther a reason to hope that the day of salvation might be near at hand. Far from being discouraged he felt that it made the imminent coming of Christ more likely.

For an understanding of Luther's social ethics it is essential to remember always that he firmly believed that all history is merely life between the times.[65] Nothing that man can do can bring about the solution of the basic problems of humanity. It is foolishness to hope for salvation from the temporal and shortsighted efforts of man. He said: "The greatest foolishness is that we fail to consider God, His judgment, His wrath, and His eternal gifts, but only concern ourselves with temporal affairs."[66] To such foolishness he did not want to be a partner. This was the reason why his

. . . .

never come. This is nothing else than to desire that the kingdom of God may not come." (Tr. Lenker)

[64] W.A.T., 5, 22, 16 ff. (5237).

[65] W.A., 12, 293, 1 (Sermons on I Peter, 1523): "This age is the last time, as St. Peter says; it will last from the ascension of Christ to the Last Day. This is why the apostles and prophets and Christ Himself call it the last hour. This does not mean that the Last Day was to come immediately after the ascension but that after this proclamation of the Gospel of Christ no other Gospel could be expected. And nothing else will be revealed and declared than what has been revealed and declared. . . . Secondly,

contemporaries found Luther slow to warm up to any world-saving schemes initiated by men. He disavowed with equal fervor the political and social panaceas of peasants and noblemen, pope and emperor. To those, for example, who placed their hope for the future upon a victory of the emperor over the Turks, he said with biting irony: "Here you can see how a poor mortal, a future victim of the worms, like the emperor, who is not sure of his life for even one moment, glorifies himself as the true protector of the Christian faith. Scripture says that Christian faith is a rock, too solid to be overthrown by the might of the devil, by death and all the powers, that this faith is a divine power (Romans 1:16). Such a power should be protected by a child of death who can be put to death by any kind of disease? Help us God, the world is crazy. . . . Well, soon we shall have a prince who will protect Christ and then someone else will protect the Holy Ghost, and then of course the Holy Trinity and Christ and Faith will be in fine shape."[67] And about the efforts of the papacy to solve man's ultimate problems by political means, he said with equal scorn: "If I were a soldier and should see as the flag of my army the colors of a cleric or a cross, even if it were a crucifix, I would run away as if the very devil were after me."[68]

Though willing to do anything in his power to help the establishment of the best possible social order in a dying

. . . .

there is not much time left to the end of the world. As St. Peter says (II Peter 3): 'One day is with the Lord as a thousand years, and a thousand years are as one day.' Thus he tries to lead us away from our own way of counting time so that we may judge time according to God's schedule. In His eyes this is the last time and the end is upon us. What is left is nothing in the eyes of God."

[66] E.A., 6, 485 ff. (Hauspostille).

[67] W.A., 15, 278, 1 (Two Imperial Decrees, 1524).

[68] W.A., 30, II, 115, 1 (On War Against the Turks, 1528).

world, he was unable to hope that this society would ever be the kingdom of God. And he rejected every effort to identify any political cause with the interest of this kingdom. Essentially he believed that even the political difficulties of man can be solved only through divine intervention. "There is no other help against the Anti-Christ devil except that the Lord Christ finally address him with the authority of His divine power, 'Get thee behind me, Satan.' "[69] And it is God who eventually brings the tyrants with all their cunning plans to naught. Luther said: "We have heard of God's great miracles which He does for His own, namely those who trust in Him and believe His Word and promise. Even if at first He acts as if He might desert them altogether so that they would be swallowed up and perish, He nevertheless comforts them and helps them in all persecution. And finally He upsets the game of the tyrants, throws away their dice, tears up their playing cards, and brings them and all their plans to naught."[70]

This firm belief in God's impending solution of all human problems is the limiting principle of Luther's social ethics. It is brilliantly summarized in a sermon on the Epistle for the Third Sunday after Easter (I Peter 2:11-20), where Luther says:

"So should Christians in all stations of life—lords and ladies, servants and maids—conduct themselves as guests on earth. Let them, in that capacity, eat and drink, make use of clothing and shoes, houses and lands, as long as God wills, yet be prepared to take up their journey when these things pass, and to move on out of this life as the guest moves on out of the house or the city which is not his home. Let them conduct themselves as does the guest, with civility toward those with whom they come in contact, not infringing on the rights of any. For a

. . . .

[69] W.A., 45, 47, 29 (Sermons, 1537).

visitor may not unrestrainedly follow his own pleasure and inclinations in the house of a stranger. The saying is: 'If you would be a guest, you must behave civilly; otherwise you may promptly be shown the door or the dungeon.' Christians should be aware of their citizenship in a better country, that they may rightly adapt themselves to this world. Let them not occupy the present life as if intending to remain in it; nor as do the monks, who flee responsibility, avoiding civil office and trying to run out of the world. For Peter says rather that we are not to escape our fellows and live each for himself, but to remain in our several callings, united with other mortals as God has bound us and serving one another. At the same time, we are to regard this life as a journey through a country where we have no citizenship—where we are not at home; to think of ourselves as travelers or pilgrims occupying for a night the same inn, eating and drinking there and then leaving the place. . . .

"Let not the occupants of the humbler stations—servants and subjects—grumble, 'Why should I vex myself with unpleasant household tasks, with farm work, or heavy labor? This life is not my home anyway, and I may as well have it better. Therefore, I will abandon my stations and enjoy myself; the monks and priests have in their stations withdrawn themselves from the world and yet drunk deeply, satisfying fleshly lusts.' No, this is not the right way. If you are unwilling to put up with your lot, as the guest in a tavern and among strangers must do, you also may not eat and drink. Similarly, they who are favored with loftier positions in life may not, upon this authority, abandon themselves to the

. . . .

[70] W.A., 16, 18, 29 (Sermons on Exodus, 1524-27).

idea of living in the sheer idleness and lustful
pleasure their more favored station permits, as if
they were to be here always. Let them reason thus:
'This life, it is true, is transitory—a voyage, a pilgrimage, leading to our actual fatherland. But since
it is God's will that everyone should serve his fellows here in his respective calling, in the office
committed to him, we will do whatever is enjoined
upon us. We will serve our subjects, our neighbors, our wives, and children so long as we can;
we would not relax our service even if we knew we
had to depart this very hour and leave all earthly
things. For, God be praised, had we to die now we

. . . .

[71] W.A., 21, 342, 37 ff. (Sommerpostille). (Tr. Lenker)

would know where we belong, where our home is. While we are here, however, on the way, it is ours to fulfill the obligations of our earthly citizenship. Therefore, we will live with our fellows in obedience to the law of our abiding place, even unto the hour wherein we must cross the threshold, that we may depart in honor, leaving no occasion for complaint.' "[71]

Thus those who have their fatherland in the coming kingdom of God pray expectantly "Thy kingdom come," knowing full well that "the kingdom of God comes indeed of itself, without our prayer; but we pray in this petition that it may come unto us also."[72]

. . . .

[72] Jacobs, *Book of Concord*, I, 368 *(Luther's Small Catechism)*.

VIII. CONCLUSION

Most discussions of Luther's social ethics are characterized by two divergent tendencies. They attempt to show either that Luther had no social ethics at all, since he placed society outside the influence of the Christian Gospel; or that his social ethics was purely pragmatic, accepting the social order of his day and thus helping to bring about the growth of capitalism and nationalism. In the preceding pages an effort has been made to free the study of Luther's thought from these artificially injected considerations and to understand his social thinking within its own context, with little regard to the part it may play in the dialectical system of some modern historian, theologian, philosopher, or economist. It has been attempted to approach Luther's social ethics not in terms of his particular views as expressed in specific historical situations but rather in terms of the principles that underlie his approach to society.

In the course of the investigation it has been shown that the claims that the Reformation or Luther created capitalism or nationalism cannot be substantiated, and that the emphasis upon the direct relationship of these great forces to the Reformation merely confuses the issue and makes the understanding of the origin of the Reformation, as well as capitalism and nationalism, more difficult. Luther's social ethics can be understood only within the framework of the principles that motivated his life and thought. It does justice neither to Luther nor to history to deal with the Reformation as if it were some metaphysical prime mover that can be used to explain the economic and political problems of our age. Luther's social thought must be understood as an integral part of his thinking and in the context of his entire approach to life.

If this road is followed, the following insights about Luther's social ethics can be gained:

I. Luther's approach to ethical problems is existential, not legal. The value of an action depends entirely upon the part it plays in helping or hindering the individual's relationship to God in Christ. All ethical standards are meaningful only in life. They are good if they serve to reveal God, and they are evil if they hide God from man. This is true of social ethics as well as individual ethics.

II. The motivating force behind all Christian ethics is God's love. Man receives God's love in faith and passes it on to the neighbor. Faith is active in love toward the neighbor. Faith brings us to Christ and makes Him our own with all that He has; then love gives us to our neighbor with all that we have.

III. God confronts all men in His Universe and demands from them obedience to the orders that He has ordained for nature. Thus not only Christians but all men are confronted by His social-ethical demands. Christian social ethics is not the esoteric teaching for the elite, but rather the God-given, i.e., best, practical way for all men to preserve the world from self-destruction until the day of Jesus Christ. Regardless of the world's attitude to the saving Gospel of Christ, it must for its own temporal preservation abide by God's natural law. Such obedience does not save man, but is conducive to the welfare of the commonwealth.

IV. The Gospel, as such, cannot be used to rule since it applies only to those who believe. It would cease to be the Gospel if it became a new law and were identified with any specific type of social organization. Yet through the person of the individual believer, who is related to Christ through the Gospel but is at the same time a member of the natural orders, faith active in love penetrates the social order. Through the Christian individual, be he peasant or prince, the inexhaustible resources of the Gospel become available to the social order.

V. All life, of individuals as well as of collectivities, is lived in the shadow of eternity. The social order is merely an interim order valid until the impending end of this world. All the ultimate problems of man's individual and social existence can be solved only when the coming kingdom of God ends all human history. Until that time, all human efforts are merely attempts to eliminate proximate evils. The ultimate evils that confront man can be overcome only through the parousia of Christ, the coming kingdom of God.

If Luther's social ethics is understood on the basis of the principles upon which it is founded, all specific answers to specific social problems of his time become relatively unimportant. They are primarily of historical rather than theological significance. However, the social ethical principles derived from Luther's existential understanding of God's revelation are of considerable interest for all those who desire to understand God's plan for the Christian in society.

Though not every specific answer that Luther gave to the problems of his age may be applicable in the modern situation, his approach will still be valid in principle. For example, confronted with the blandishments of the Turks, who wanted to use him and his movement against the papacy, and at the same time faced with the appeals of the empire, under the influence of the papacy, to use his power on behalf of a Christian crusade against the pagan Turks, Luther declined both invitations on the basis of his Christian conviction that the end never justifies the means. Here Luther's stand sheds some light upon the contemporary dilemma of evangelical Christianity called to choose between the totalitarianism of Moscow and Rome, for the sake of expediency.

Similarly, Luther's objection to all attempts to make the Gospel the law of the Christian state seems equally valid and urgent in our time.

Though he erred in expecting the end of the world in his time, acceptance of his emphasis upon the finiteness of all human efforts to solve even man's social predicament could have saved many an upright and noble man who in our time trusted in human solutions much anguish and despair.

Living his faith in love, Luther tried all during his life to bring his personal Christian witness to bear upon the decisions that confronted his society. From the ninety-five theses of Wittenberg to the quarrel of the counts of Mannsfeld at Eisleben, he never tired of living his social ethics, showing in his own life that through the Christian individual the Gospel penetrates the social order. It would have been well for Christendom if those who followed Luther's lead had been equally zealous to show their faith active in love.

IX. BIBLIOGRAPHY

Primary Sources

Book of Concord, The Symbolical Books of the Evangelical Lutheran Church, edited and translated by Henry E. Jacobs, 2 vols., Philadelphia, 1908.

Luther, Martin, *Ausgewählte Werke,* edited by Hans Heinrich Borcherdt, Munich, 1922-25.

Luther, Martin, *Briefwechsel,* Kritische Gesamtausgabe, vol. I ff., Weimar, 1930 ff.

Luther, Martin, *Correspondence and Other Contemporary Letters,* edited and translated by Preserved Smith and C. M. Jacobs, 2 vols., Philadelphia, 1913-18.

Luther, Martin, *House-Postil,* edited by M. Loy, 2 vols., Columbus, 1869-1871.

Luther, Martin, *Sämtliche Schriften,* herausgegeben von Dr. Johann Georg Walch, neue revidierte Stereotypausgabe, 23 vols., St. Louis, 1880-1910.

Luther, Martin, *Sämtliche Werke,* 67 vols., Erlangen, 1826-57.

Luther, Martin, *The Precious and Sacred Writings of Dr. Martin Luther,* edited by J. N. Lenker, 14 volumes, Minneapolis, 1905.

Luther, Martin, *The Table-Talk,* translated by William Hazlitt, London, 1902.

Luther, Martin, *Tischreden,* Kritische Gesamtausgabe, 6 vols., Weimar, 1912-21.

Luther, Martin, *Werke,* Kritische Gesamtausgabe, 56 vols., Weimar, 1883 ff.

Luther, Martin, *Works,* with introductions and notes, 6 vols., Philadelphia, 1915-32.

Allen, J. W., *History of Political Thought in the Sixteenth Century*, New York, 1928.

Althaus, Paul, *Staatsgedanke und Reich Gottes*, Langensalza, 1926.

    Theologie der Ordnungen, Gütersloh, 1935.

    Luther und die Politik, Gütersloh, 1940.

    Luthers Haltung im Bauernkrieg, Basel, post-1945 (no date).

    An Outline of Ethics, translated by A. B. Little, S. T. D. dissertation, Chicago Lutheran Theological Seminary, 1948.

Ante-Nicene Fathers, edited by A. Roberts and J. Donaldson, 10 vols., Grand Rapids, 1950-51.

The Apostolic Fathers, with an English translation by Kirsopp Lake, 2 vols., Cambridge, 1912.

The Student's Oxford Aristotle, translated by W. D. Ross, London, 1942.

Arnold, Franz Xavier, *Zur Frage des Naturrechts bei Martin Luther*, Munich, 1937.

Aulen, Gustaf, *Den kristna gudsbilden genom seklerna och i nutiden*, Stockholm, 1927.

    Christus Victor, London, 1931.

Baillie, D. M., *God Was in Christ*, New York, 1948.

Bainton, Roland H., *Here I Stand*, New York, 1950.

    The Reformation of the Sixteenth Century, Boston, 1952.

Barge, Hermann, *Andreas Bodenstein von Karlstadt*, 2 vols., Leipzig, 1905.

    Luther und der Frühkapitalismus, Gütersloh, 1951.

Barth, Karl, *Die protestantische Theologie im 19. Jahrhundert*, Zürich, 1947.

Bennett, John C., *Christian Ethics and Social Policy*, New York, 1946.

Berggrav, Eivind, *Man and State*, Philadelphia, 1951.

Betcke, Werner, *Luthers Sozialethik*, Gütersloh, 1934.

Betzendörfer, Walter, *Glauben und Wissen bei den Grossen Denkern des Mittelalters*, Gotha, 1931.

Billing, Einar, *Luthers lära om staten*, Uppsala, 1900.

    Our Calling, translated by Conrad Bergendoff, Rock Island, Illinois, 1947.

Binder, Julius, *Luthers Staatsauffassung,* Berlin, 1918.

Boehmer, Heinrich, *Luther and the Reformation in the Light of Modern Research,* translated by E. S. G. Potter, London, 1930.

Road to Reformation, translated by J. W. Doberstein and T. G. Tappert, Philadelphia, 1946.

Brandenburg, Erich, *Martin Luthers Anschauung von Staat und Gesellschaft,* Halle, 1901.

Brentano, Lujo, *Die Anfänge des modernen Kapitalismus,* Munich, 1916.

Der wirtschaftende Mensch in der Geschichte, Leipzig, 1923.

Bring, Ragnar, *Dualismen hos Luther,* Lund, 1929.

Förhallandet mellan tro och gärningar inom luthersk teologi, Lund, 1933.

Brunner, Emil, *The Divine Imperative,* translated by Olive Wyon, London, 1937.

Calvin, John, *Institutes of the Christian Religion,* translated by John Allen, 2 vols., Philadelphia, 1936.

Cambridge Medieval History, edited by H. M. Gwatkin and J. P. Whitney, 8 vols., New York, 1924-36.

Cambridge Modern History, 12 vols., New York, 1903-10.

Carlson, Edgar M., *The Reinterpretation of Luther,* Philadelphia, 1948.

Catlin, George, *The Story of the Political Philosophers,* New York, 1939.

Cave, Sidney, *The Doctrine of the Person of Christ,* London, 1925.

Clemen, Otto, *Flugschriften aus den ersten Jahren der Reformation,* Halle, 1906.

Creighton, M., *A History of the Papacy,* New York, 1901.

Denifle, H., *Luther in rationalistischer und christlicher Beleuchtung* Mainz, 1904.

Luther und Lutherthum, 2 vols., Mainz, 1904-09.

Deutelmoser, Arno, *Luther, Staat und Glaube,* Jena, 1937.

Diem, Harald, *Luthers Lehre von den zwei Reichen,* Munich, 1938.

Dittrich, Ottmar, *Luthers Ethik in ihren Grundzügen dargestellt,* Leipzig, 1930.

Dörries, Hermann, *Luther und Deutschland,* Tübingen, 1934.

Eger, Karl, *Die Anschauung Luthers vom Beruf,* Giessen, 1900.

Ehrenberg, Richard, *Das Zeitalter der Fugger,* 2 vols., Jena, 1895.

Elert, Werner, *Morphologie des Luthertums,* 2 vols., Munich, 1932.

    Das christliche Ethos, Tübingen, 1949.

Ellwein, Eduard, *Vom neuen Leben,* Munich, 1932.

Erhardt, Eugene, *La notion du droit naturel chez Luther,* Paris, 1901.

Evans, Austin P., *An Episode in the Struggle for Religious Freedom,* New York, 1924.

Fanfani, Amintore, *Catholicism, Protestantism, and Capitalism,* London, 1934.

Forell, George W., *The Reality of the Church as the Communion of Saints,* Wenonah, New Jersey, 1943.

    "Luther and the War Against the Turks," *Church History,* XIV, 4, 1945.

    "Luther's View Concerning the Imperial Foreign Policy," *The Lutheran Quarterly,* IV, 2, 1952.

Franz, Günther, *Der deutsche Bauernkrieg,* Munich, 1933.

Genrich, P. W., *Die Christologie Luthers im Abendmahlsstreit,* Göttingen, 1929.

Gibbon, Edward, *The History of the Decline and Fall of the Roman Empire,* 6 vols., New York, 1900.

Gogarten, Friedrich, *Politische Ethik,* Jena, 1932.

Grimm, Harold J., "Luther and the Peasant Revolt," *Lutheran Church Quarterly,* XIX, 2, 1946.

Grisar, Hartman, *Luther,* 3 vols., Freiburg, 1911.

Gyllenkrok, Axel, *Rechtfertigung und Heiligung,* Uppsala, 1952.

Hall, George F., "Luther's Eschatology," *The Augustana Quarterly,* XXIII, 1944.

Harkness, Georgia, *John Calvin, the Man and his Ethics,* New York, 1931.

Harnack, Adolf, *Martin Luther in seiner Bedeutung für die Geschichte der Wissenschaft und der Bildung,* Giessen, 1883.

Harnack, Theodosius, *Luthers Theologie,* 2 vols., Munich, 1926.

Heim, Karl, *Das Gewissheitsproblem in der systematischen Theologie bis zu Schleiermacher,* Leipzig, 1911.

Heimann, Eduard, *Freedom and Order,* New York, 1947.

Hendry, George S., *God the Creator,* Nashville, 1938.

Herzog, J. J., *Real-Encyklopädie für protestantische Theologie und Kirche,* Leipzig, 1877-88.

Hirsch, Emmanuel, *Luthers Gottesanschauung,* Göttingen, 1918.

Holl, Karl, *Gesammelte Aufsätze zur Kirchengeschichte,* 3 vols., Tübingen, 1923.

Holstein, Günther, *Luther und die deutsche Staatsidee,* Tübingen, 1926.

Holsten, Walter, "Reformation und Mission," *Archiv für Reformationsgeschichte,* XLIV, 1, 1953.

Introduction to Contemporary Civilization in the West, prepared by the staff of Columbia College, 2 vols., New York, 1946.

Janssen, Johannes, *History of the German People at the Close of the Middle Ages,* London, 1896, 1925.

Joachimsen, Paul, *Sozialethik des Luthertums,* Munich, 1927.

Jordan, Herrmann, *Luthers Staatsauffassung,* Munich, 1917.

Jorgensen, Alfred Th., *Filantropi,* Copenhagen, 1939.

Kantonen, Taito A., *Resurgence of the Gospel,* Philadelphia, 1948.

Kautsky, Karl, *Communism in Central Europe in the Time of the Reformation,* London, 1897.

Kinder, Ernst, *Geistliches und weltliches Regiment Gottes nach Luther,* Weimar, 1940.

Köberle, Adolf, *The Quest for Holiness,* Minneapolis, 1938.

Köhler, Walther E., *Luthers Schrift 'An den christlichen Adel deutscher Nation,'* Halle, 1895.
    Dokumente zum Ablassstreit, Tübingen, 1902.
    Luther und Luthertum in ihrer weltgeschichtlichen Auswirkung, Leipzig, 1903.

Kolde, Theodor, *Der Staatsgedanke der Reformation und die römische Kirche,* Leipzig, 1903.

Köstlin, Julius, *Luthers Theologie,* 2 vols., Stuttgart, 1901.

Lamparter, Helmut, *Luthers Stellung zum Türkenkrieg,* Munich, 1940.

Lau, Franz, *Aüsserliche Ordnung und Weltlich Ding in Luthers Theologie,* Göttingen, 1933.
    Luthers Lehre von den beiden Reichen, Berlin, 1953.

Lewin, R., *Luthers Stellung zu den Juden,* Berlin, 1911.

Lilje, Hanns, *Luther Now,* Philadelphia, 1952.

Lindsay, Thomas, *A History of the Reformation,* 2 vols., New York, 1926.

Link, Wilhelm, *Das Ringen Luthers um die Freiheit der Theologie von der Philosophie,* Munich, 1940.

Ljungren, Gustaf, *Zur Geschichte der christlichen Heilsgewissheit von Augustin bis zur Hochscholastik,* Uppsala, 1920.
Synd och skuld i Luthers teologi, Uppsala, 1928.

Lortz, Joseph, *Die Reformation in Deutschland,* 2 vols., Freiburg, 1949.

Luchaire, Achille, *Social France at the Time of Philip Augustus,* translated by Edward B. Krehbiel, New York, 1912.

Lunt, William E., *Papal Revenues in the Middle Ages,* New York, 1934.

Luthard, Ernst, *Die Ethik Luthers in ihren Grundzügen,* Leipzig, 1867.

Maritain, Jacques, *Three Reformers,* London, 1928.

Matthes, Kurt, *Das Corpus Christianum bei Luther,* Berlin, 1929.

McGovern, William M., *From Luther to Hitler,* Boston, 1941.

McNeill, John T., *Unitive Protestantism,* Nashville, 1930.
Christian Hope for World Society, Chicago, 1937.
"Natural Law in the Thought of Luther," *Church History,* X, 3, 1941.

Miller, Edward W. and Jared W. Scudder, *Wessel Gansfort, Life and Writings,* 2 vols., New York, 1917.

Mirbt, Carl, *Quellen zur Geschichte des Papsttums und des-römischen Katholizismus,* 3rd ed., Tübingen, 1911.

Müller, Karl, *Kirche, Gemeinde und Obrigkeit nach Luther,* Tübingen, 1910.

Nathusius, Martin von, *Die Mitarbeit der Kirche an der Lösung der sozialen Frage,* Leipzig, 1904.

Nelson, Benjamin N., *The Idea of Usury,* Princeton, 1949.

Nicene and Post-Nicene Fathers, edited by Philip Schaff, 2 series, 28 vols., Buffalo, 1886 ff.

Niebuhr, H. Richard, *Christ and Culture,* New York, 1951.

Niebuhr, Reinhold, *The Nature and Destiny of Man,* 2 vols., New York, 1941-43.
The Children of Light and the Children of Darkness, New York, 1946.
Faith and History, New York, 1949.

Nygren, Anders, *Agape and Eros,* 2 parts, 3 vols., London, 1932-39.

Obendiek, Harmannus, *Der Teufel bei Martin Luther,* Berlin, 1931.

Olsson, Herbert, *Grundproblemet i Luthers socialetik,* Lund, 1934.

Pelikan, Jaroslav, *From Luther to Kierkegaard,* St. Louis, 1950.

Pfeffermann, H., *Die Zusammenarbeit der Renaisancepäpste mit den Türken,* Winterthur, 1946.

Pinomaa, Lennart, *Der existentielle Character der Theologie Luthers,* Helsinki, 1940.

Prenter, Regin, *Spiritus Creator,* translated by J. M. Jensen, Philadelphia, 1953.

Preuss, Hans, *Die Vorstellung vom Antichrist im späteren Mittelalter bei Luther und in der konfessionellen Polemik,* Leipzig, 1906.

Preus, Herman A., *The Communion of Saints,* Minneapolis, 1948.

Ranke, Leopold von, *History of the Popes,* London, 1852.
History of the Reformation in Germany, translated by Sarah Austin, London, 1905.

Robertson, Hector M., *Aspects of the Rise of Economic Individualism,* Cambridge, 1933.

Rommen, Heinrich A., *The Natural Law,* St. Louis, 1949.

Rupp, Gordon, *Martin Luther, Hitler's Cause or Cure,* London, 1945.
The Righteousness of God, New York, 1953.

Schapiro, Jacob S., *Social Reform and the Reformation,* New York, 1909.

Schilling, Otto, *Die Staats und Soziallehre des hl. Augustinus,* Freiburg, 1910.

Schöffel, J. S. and Adolf Köberle, *Luthertum und soziale Frage,* Leipzig, 1931.

Schneider, Ernst, *Martin Luther, sexualethische Anweisungen,* Kandern, 1926.

Schulte, Aloys, *Die Fugger in Rom, 1495-1523,* 2 vols., Leipzig, 1904.

Schwiebert, Ernest G., "The Reformation from a New Perspective," *Church History,* XVII, 1, 1948.
Luther and his Times, St. Louis, 1951.

Seeberg, Erich, *Luthers Theologie,* vol. I, Göttingen, 1929, vol. 2, Stuttgart, 1937.

Seeberg, Reinhold, *Aus Religion und Geschichte,* vol. I, Leipzig, 1906.

"Luthers Anschauung von dem Geschlechtsleben und der Ehe," *Luther Jahrbuch,* Wittenberg, 1925.

Sittler, Joseph, *The Doctrine of the Word,* Philadelphia, 1948.

Smith, Preserved, *The Age of the Reformation,* New York, 1920.

Sohm, Rudolf, *Kirchenrecht,* Leipzig, vol. I, 1892, vol. II, 1922.

Sormunen, Eino, *Die Eigenart der lutherischen Ethik,* Helsinki, 1934.

Spitz, Lewis W., "Luther's Ecclesiology and his Concept of the Prince as Notbischof," *Church History,* XXII, 2, 1953.

Stange, Carl, *Studien zur Theologie Luthers,* Gütersloh, 1928.

Steinlein, Herman, *Luther und der Bauernkrieg,* Munich, 1903.

Stephan, Horst, *Luther in den Wandlungen seiner Kirche,* Giessen, 1907.

Stomps, M. A. H., *Die Anthropologie Martin Luthers,* Frankfurt, 1935.

Stratenwerth, Günter, *Die Naturrechtslehre des Johannes Duns Scotus,* Göttingen, 1951.

Switalski, Bruno, *Neo-Platonism and the Ethics of St. Augustine,* New York, 1946.

Tawney, R. H., *Religion and the Rise of Capitalism,* New York, 1926.

Thielicke, Helmut, *Theologische Ethik,* vol. I, Tübingen, 1951.

Thomas Aquinas, *Summa Theologica,* translated by Fathers of the English Dominican province, 22 vols., London, 1920.

Toynbee, Arnold J., *A Study of History,* 6 vols., London, 1935.

Treitschke, Heinrich von, *Luther und die Deutsche Nation,* Berlin, 1883.

Troeltsch, Ernst, *The Social Teachings of the Christian Churches,* translated by Olive Wyon, 2 vols., London, 1931.

Törnvall, Gustaf, *Andligt och världsligt regemente hos Luther,* Stockholm, 1940.

Vogelsang, Erich, *Luthers Kampf gegen die Juden,* Tübingen, 1933.

Walser, Fritz, *Die politische Entwicklung Ulrichs von Hutten,* Berlin, 1928.

Waring, Luther Hess, *The Political Theories of Martin Luther,* New York, 1910.

Watson, Philip S., *Let God be God,* Philadelphia, 1948.

Weber, Max, *Gesammelte Aufsätze zur Religionssoziologie,* 3 vols., Tübingen, 1922.

The Protestant Ethic and the Spirit of Capitalism, New York, 1930.

Wiener, Peter F., *Martin Luther, Hitler's Spiritual Ancestor,* London, 1945.

Wingren, Gustaf, *Luthers lära om kallelsen,* Lund, 1942.

Winter, Ernst Karl, *Die Sozialmetaphysik der Scholastik,* Vienna, 1929.

Wolf, Ernst, Politia Christi, *Evangelische Theologie,* vol. VIII, 1948-49.

"Zur Frage des Naturrechts bei Thomas von Aquin und bei Luther," *Jahrbuch der Gesellschaft für die Geschichte des Protestantismus in Oesterreich,* LXVII, Vienna, 1951.

Wolff, Otto, *Haupttypen der neueren Lutherdeutung,* Stuttgart, 1938.

Wünsch, Georg, *Der Zusammenbruch des Luthertums als Sozialgestaltung,* Tübingen, 1921.

Evangelische Wirtschaftsethik, Tübingen, 1927.

Evangelische Ethik des Politischen, Tübingen, 1936.

ABOUT THE AUTHOR

George W. Forell was born in Breslau, Germany, the son, grandson, and great-grandson of Protestant clergymen. After studying philosophy and theology at the University of Vienna, he came to the United States in 1939 to continue his studies at the Lutheran Theological Seminary in Philadelphia. After his ordination as a pastor of the Lutheran church, he served parishes in New Jersey and in New York City, continuing at the same time his studies at Princeton Theological Seminary and, later, at Union Theological Seminary. From the latter he received the degree of Doctor of Theology.

Dr. Forell has been a member of the philosophy department at Gustavus Adolphus College, St. Peter, Minn., and professor of systematic theology at Chicago Lutheran Theological Seminary. He has been a guest professor at the theological faculty of the University of Hamburg, Germany, and the All-Africa Theological Seminary at Marangu, Tanganyika. At present he is professor of Protestant theology in the School of Religion of the State University of Iowa, Iowa City.

Other books by Dr. Forell are *The Reality of the Church as the Communion of Saints, Ethics of Decision,* and *The Protestant Faith.* He is the editor of Volume 32 of *The American Edition of Luther's Works* and a past president of the American Society for Reformation Research.